W9-ANO-275

With the compliments
of the Canada Council

Avec les hommages
du Conseil des Arts
du Canada

Building the Rideau Canal:
A Pictorial History

"Give and Forgive"
By Family Motto

Building the Rideau Canal:
A PICTORIAL HISTORY

Robert W. Passfield

Published by
Fitzhenry & Whiteside
in association with Parks Canada

 Parks   Parcs
Canada   Canada

Front Cover: Kingston Mills, post 1856
Thomas Burrowes; watercolour, 6⅜" × 10"
Archives of Ontario

Back cover: Royal Sappers and Miners, 1825
George B. Campion

Cover design: Don Fernley

© Crown copyrights reserved.

© Minister of Supply and Services Canada, 1982.
   Published by Fitzhenry & Whiteside Limited
   150 Lesmill Road
   Don Mills, Ontario, Canada M3B 2T5

Canadian Cataloguing in Publication Data
Passfield, Robert W. (Robert Walter), 1942-
   Building the Rideau Canal
Issued also in French under title: Construction du
canal Rideau.
Bibliography: p.
ISBN 0-88902-706-4

1. Rideau Canal (Ont.) — History. I. Title.
HE401.R5P37   386'.5'097137   C82-094482-3

Printed in Canada

Contents

Preface

Parks Canada is publishing this book to celebrate the 150th anniversary of the building of the Rideau Canal. It traces the efforts of the British Army Ordnance Department to bring the canal into being and tells how Lieutenant Colonel John By struggled to complete the project in the face of a forbidding landscape and a cost-conscious, sometimes hostile government in London. The triumphant completion of the canal is set against By's own official disgrace in an effort to illuminate, if not remove, some of the controversy that still surrounds his name 150 years after the event.

Colonel By was praised for completing one of the greatest engineering projects of the 19th century and admired for the quality of its workmanship, yet he was branded an incompetent by the Treasury and accused of spending unauthorized monies. More recently, By has been portrayed as a man of great ambition who, to satisfy his personal designs and grandiose plans, deliberately misled his superiors through guile, evasiveness and careless reports, and tricked them into permitting the construction of a much larger, more costly canal than planned; a man who by squandering large sums of money, inflated the cost of the canal five-fold over the preliminary estimate. Such actions, it has been asserted, drew the wrath of the Treasury down upon By and the Ordnance Department with disastrous results for the security of the Canadas in that monies were not forthcoming for the completion of the Ordnance's plan of defence, and the huge expenditures on the canal were supposedly largely wasted. The research on which the present book is based totally contradicts that view. By emerges as a man dreadfully wronged, an officer and a gentleman, and a highly competent engineer who was responsible for providing Upper Canada with a viable system of defence at the cost of his health and career.

This pictorial history is based on four years of research on the subject of the Rideau Canal and draws substantially on the author's heavily documented manuscript: *Engineering the Defence of the Canadas: Lt. Col. John By and the Rideau Canal* (Manuscript Report Series No. 425, Parks Canada; on deposit in the Public Archives of Canada and the provincial archives).

This book takes advantage of a superb collection of watercolours and sketches produced by the Royal Engineers and contemporary military topographers. It will bring before the public reproductions of art works that are widely scattered in numerous holdings: The Agnes Etherington Art Centre, Queen's University at Kingston; the Chateau Laurier, Canadian National Hotels, Ottawa; the Dalhousie Muniments, Scottish Record Office, Edinburgh, Scotland; the McCord Museum, McGill University, Montreal; the Archives of Ontario, Toronto; the Public Archives of Canada, Ottawa; the Public Record Office, London, England; The Royal Commonwealth Society, London, England, and the Royal Ontario Museum, Toronto.

The watercolours and sketches generally focus on the locksites. Only Lieutenant Colonel James Patterson Cockburn, who toured the Rideau in August 1830, consistently chose as his subjects the untouched landscape and the nascent pre-canal settlements. The book presents only a selection of the Rideau Canal watercolours and sketches by James Cockburn, various members of By's engineering staff and officers who were on the canal at a later date, and by no means represents all of the military topographers who drew Rideau subjects. The illustrations were selected to show how the canal was constructed, the nature of the difficulties overcome, and the works actually erected, rather than exclusively for artistic merit or their representa-

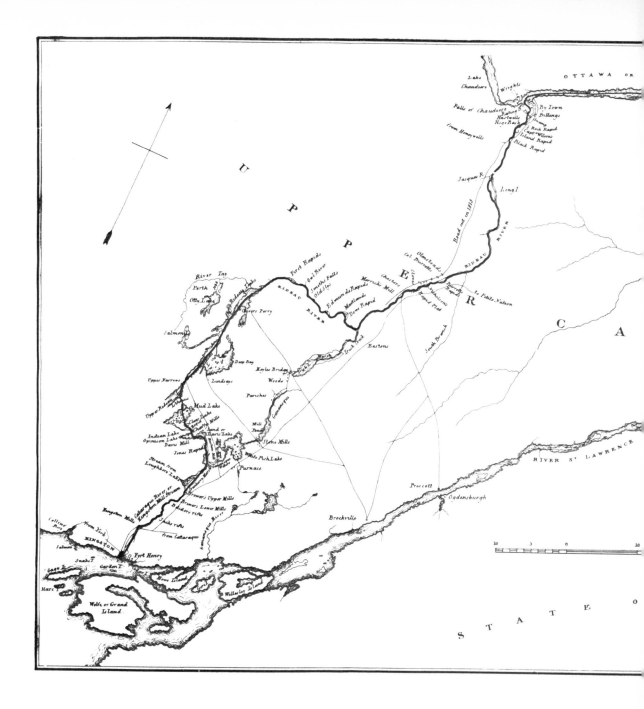

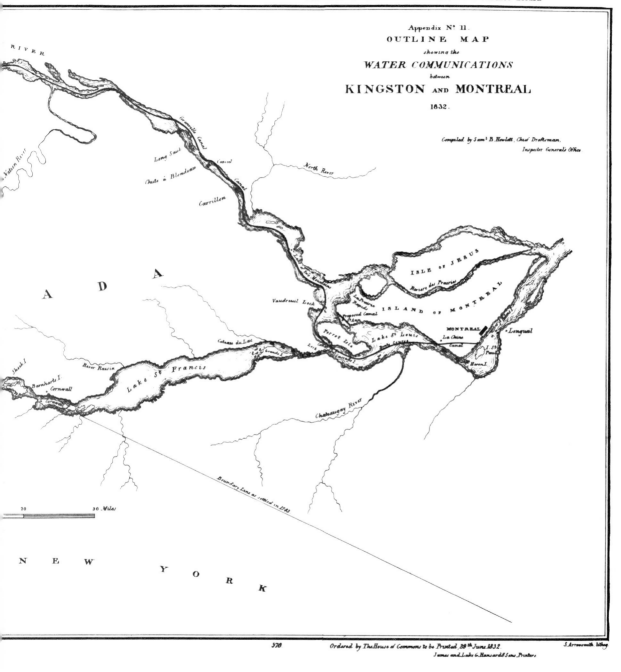

Appendix N° 11.

OUTLINE MAP

showing the

WATER COMMUNICATIONS

between

KINGSTON AND MONTREAL

1832.

Compiled by Saml. B. Hewlett, Chief Draftsman.
Inspector Generals Office.

RIVER

Nation River

North River

Grenville Canal

Long Saut

Chute à Blondeau

Carillon

Cascal

Canal

ISLE OF JESUS

Riviere des Prairies

ISLAND OF MONTREAL

Vaudreuil Lock

MONTREAL

La Chine Canal

Longueil

A D A

Coteau du Lac

River Raisin

Lake Grande

Perrot Isle

Lake St. Louis

I. St. Paul

Lake St. Francis

Chateaugay River

Barnharts I.

Cornwall

Sheek I.

Boundary Line as settled in 1783

N E W   Y O R K

20   30 Miles

9

tional value with respect to a particular school or artist. Hence the inclusion of works by several civilian artists such as Edwin Whitefield (1816-1892), an itinerant English watercolourist, and C. W. Jeffreys (1869-1952), a Canadian artist of a much later date. The watercolours and sketches, however, are for the most part of high quality and merit reproduction as art works in their own right.

The author is indebted to his colleagues at the National Historic Parks and Sites Branch, Parks Canada, who have written on the subject of the Rideau Canal, and Mrs. Jean Burgess, Research Information Section, and Jean Brathwaite, Research Publications Section, who helped immeasurably in the preparation of this book.

Robert W. Passfield
Parks Canada
October 1981

Introduction

The Rideau Canal was built to defend the Canadas against invasion from the United States. Connecting the Ottawa River with Kingston on Lake Ontario, the canal was intended to provide a secure interior water route for moving British troops from the ocean ports of Quebec and Montreal to the defence of Upper Canada (Ontario). The War of 1812 showed that the St. Lawrence River supply route to Upper Canada was extremely vulnerable to American attack and the Rideau system was a key element in a much larger defence scheme formulated by the Duke of Wellington, the Master General of the British Army Ordnance Department, that required the construction of a series of fortifications at key positions in Upper and Lower Canada, interconnected by a network of interior canals.

The Rideau Canal, constructed between 1826 and 1832, was a child of the Ordnance Department. The Ordnance promoted the canal, selected Lieutenant Colonel By to superintend its construction, and operated the finished waterway until 1856 when, in the waning days of the department, the canal and surrounding Ordnance lands were turned over to the provincial government of the united Canadas. The canal began as a modest proposal for moving small bateaux across the river systems of the Rideau interior using a few wooden locks and dams. By the time it was completed, the Rideau was a waterway of 47 masonry locks and accompanying dams stretching across 123 miles of Upper Canadian wilderness. The finished canal included several engineering feats unequalled anywhere in the world and cost the British Treasury more than any other military construction project in the entire British Empire to that time.

When it was finished the Rideau Canal played a major role in the Canadian commercial transport system and was largely responsible for the settlement and development of the Rideau interior. As well, it was the critical military supply route on which the survival of Upper Canada depended in the event of war, the basis of a revolutionary new defence strategy, and the first steamboat canal to be constructed anywhere.

Origin of the Rideau Project

Supplying an Army on the Frontier

It is wholly impossible to supply the Forces . . . .
Commissary General Robinson
14 November 1814

In June 1812, the United States declared war on Great Britain. Despite its name, the War of 1812 actually lasted two and a half years. During that time the Canadian colonies were under constant threat of invasion by the Americans. Several attacks were launched, by land and by water, but soldiers of the British army, supported by Indian allies and the local militia, were equal to the challenge until finally, late in 1814, peace was restored.

During the War of 1812 the greatest difficulty faced by the British army was the inadequacy of the St. Lawrence River transport system, the sole artery by which troops, ordnance and supplies could be moved to Upper Canada from the ocean ports of Quebec and Montreal in Lower Canada. By 1814 the ever-increasing demands being placed on the transport system strained its shipping capacity and manpower to the breaking point and threatened to make military operations in Upper Canada impossible.

On the St. Lawrence, heavy freight going up river had to be carted overland eight miles from Montreal to Lachine, at the head of Montreal Island, to avoid the Lachine rapids. At Lachine, cargoes were loaded into flat-bottomed bateaux for shipment up the river to Kingston on Lake Ontario. This 120-mile passage was extremely difficult. On the Upper St. Lawrence there were three relatively long, quiet stretches of water where bateaux could proceed by oar or sail, but they were separated by two nine-mile-long series of rapids where the river narrowed and the water ran so swiftly that bateaux were unable to make headway. At the base of each series of rapids, cargoes had to be transhipped into ox carts while the lightened bateaux were laboriously poled through the rough water. Three short canals helped the crews to avoid part of the first set of rapids, and occasionally oxen were able to tow the bateaux along shore, but otherwise progress was slow and exhausting. Once clear of the upper rapids, the bateaux were fully loaded again to sail the last 67 miles to Kingston where they would arrive anywhere from 11 to 14 days after leaving Lachine. The return voyage, on which the bateaux were able to shoot the rapids, required only three to four days.

The St. Lawrence transport system functioned reasonably well in the prewar period, but the unprecedented heavy transport demands of the military during the war altered the situation dramatically. Upper Canada was a sparsely settled, heavily forested frontier area where the bulk of the population lived by subsistence agriculture. Consequently, in wartime all of the ordnance, munitions, and food rations required to sustain an army had to be imported via the St. Lawrence. Moreover, as of 1813 American and British forces fighting on the Upper Canadian frontier had begun a shipbuilding war for naval supremacy on Lake Ontario which required the Ordnance Department to bring up the St. Lawrence all of the heavy guns, anchors and ship cables that the Royal Navy needed to equip the 100-gun warships being constructed in the Kingston dockyard.

The Ordnance increased the capacity of the existing forwarding system. The prewar bateaux establishment of 25 vessels grew to the point where at the height of the war some 200 bateaux a week were proceeding up river from Lachine, and farmers from as far as 30 miles distant were being called out on corvée duty with their ox teams and carts to man the portages. This was enormously costly. As many as 10,000 men, including 3500 bateauxmen, had to be employed on the St. Lawrence at one time or another, and the Ordnance saw its annual expenditure triple in three years to £341,000. It was obvious by the close of the 1814 navigation season that the growing manpower shortage would make it impossible to maintain the transport system at its 1814 capacity, let alone expand it further. Consequently, the local Commissariat planned improvements so that more cargo could be transported in less time by fewer hands. But before these improvements were begun, it was learned that the Americans, who had been slow to recognize the strategic importance and highly vulnerable nature of the St. Lawrence system, were planning to focus their military and naval resources in an effort to cut that link during the 1815 campaign.

Logistics were determining the course of the struggle. Time and again, offensive operations were aborted by one army or the other when it proved impossible to transport sufficient supplies either to launch a large-scale attack or to sustain it. Both sides came to recognize the critical importance of supply, and the struggle for naval supremacy on Lake Ontario was but a belated recognition of this crucial factor.

British forces were at a decided disadvantage. Not only did all war material have to be imported from England and transported up the tortuously slow and costly St. Lawrence route, but this sole line of supply, was exceedingly difficult to defend for it lay exposed along the whole of the fighting front. In contrast, most American supply lines consisted of excellent water communications stretching back in relative security from the fighting front to manufacturing and farming centres in the rear. If the Americans were resolved to cut the St. Lawrence communication, the prospect of continuing to supply the British forces in Upper Canada by that route appeared all but hopeless.

The Rideau Alternative

It is quite impracticable . . . .
Quarter Master General Nicol
7 January 1815

With their supply lines and frontier army at risk, British military authorities in November 1814 launched a search for an alternative route through the interior. The first proposal was a scheme suggested by Lieutenant Colonel George Macdonnel, a Canadian serving with the British army, who recommended that a water route be opened across the height of land dividing Lake Ontario and the Ottawa River Valley, linking a number of rivers and small lakes in the Lake Ontario watershed north of Kingston with water flowing into the Rideau River in the Ottawa River watershed. Bateaux ascending the Ottawa from Montreal could then pass through the interior of Upper Canada to Kingston in perfect security.

As early as 1783 the government had despatched small parties to examine the Cataraqui and Gananoque rivers in the Lake Ontario watershed and the Rideau River and its Irish Creek tributary to determine whether the adjacent lands were suitable for settlement, but only in the following decade had a number of settlers cut their way inland to establish small, isolated settlements at waterfalls on the Rideau and Irish Creek. Little was yet known about the extent of the headwaters of the Rideau River, but after conversing with the Rideau settlers serving in militia units on the St. Lawrence front, Macdonnel became convinced that a water route through the Rideau interior to Kingston was feasible.

After reconnoitring the rivers of the Rideau interior himself, Macdonnel reported in December 1814 that a bateaux navigation could be formed by connecting the headwaters of the Cataraqui River, which entered Lake Ontario at Kingston, with the Rideau River via either its

Rideau Lakes headwaters or its Irish Creek branch. Macdonnel proposed to construct a small number of temporary timber-crib dams and wooden locks to improve the rivers sufficiently to permit the passage of loaded bateaux. Portages would connect the separate bodies of navigable water. He was convinced that a system could be constructed via the Rideau Lakes for as little as £25,000 and completed in time for the 1815 campaign.

Objections focussed on the large number of lengthy portages. Not only would they slow transport to a crawl, but also require a large and costly complement of men and oxen which could not be sustained in the heavily-forested Rideau interior where there was no forage for draught animals.

However, the American threat overcame all objections. Sir George Prevost, Commander of the Forces, decided to begin work on a Rideau bateaux system as soon as possible in the spring of 1815. He sent a surveyor to explore the interior waterways to establish the location of portages, locks and dams, as well as the cost of building them and where to procure the necessary oxen. The surveyor agreed with Macdonnel that a bateaux route was practicable. He recommended changes in routing and assured Prevost that the proposed navigation would deliver bateaux from the Ottawa River to Kingston as quickly as they made the trip up the St. Lawrence, exclusive of the time required to reach the mouth of the Rideau from Montreal. However, whether it would be as inexpensive and efficient as he predicted remained an unanswered question. News was received that Britain and the United States had signed a peace treaty and the immediate threat to the safety of the Canadas disappeared.

In Defence of Canada

The possession of [the St. Lawrence] . . . . ought not to be ours for three days after the commencement of hostilities.

Duke of Richmond
10 November 1818

Although the end of the war removed the serious logistical problems facing the Ordnance, it did not result in the shelving of the Rideau project. The United States was still a potential threat and local British military commanders were convinced that the security of the Canadas was dependent in large measure on developing a water communication with Upper Canada independent of the St. Lawrence. As a result, the Duke of Richmond, the Governor-in-Chief, evolved an ambitious plan that included a citadel at Quebec to secure the landing of British troops coming to aid the standing garrisons, a fort at Isle aux Noix to defend the Lake Champlain-Richelieu River invasion route from the south, and a new stronghold at Kingston. The Rideau project, along with a canal to Lachine and several short canals on the Ottawa River, was necessary to provide a secure and efficient water communication with Kingston. The plan further called for discharged war veterans and British immigrants to be settled in the wilderness of the Rideau interior to provide militia units to defend that all-important inland communication.

Efforts to get the navigations under construction began in 1816 when Lieutenant Joshua Jebb of the Corps of Royal Engineers was despatched to survey and map the rapids on the Irish Creek route.

Jebb found a five-foot depth of water on the navigable stretches of the Rideau, Irish Creek and Cataraqui waterways, and concluded that most of the system could be rendered navigable for bateaux with minor improvements in the rapids and the construction of a few locks. The Rideau River below Long Island presented a more difficult challenge as the rapids were exceptionally wide and shallow. Here Jebb suggested that wing walls be constructed to contract and deepen the channel and capstans be erected to enable the crews to winch their boats through. On the whole system from the Ottawa River to Kingston, only two portages were necessary: at the Rideau Falls, where the Rideau River fell 30 feet into the Ottawa River, and at the five-mile-wide summit between Irish Creek and the headwaters of the Cataraqui River.

Initially, it was planned to improve the Ottawa-Rideau system just enough to permit the passage of fully laden bateaux through the rapids with as little portaging as possible. However Durham boats were just coming into widespread use as an alternative to bateaux on larger rivers. Durham boats were 20 feet longer and five feet wider than the 40-foot-by-six-foot bateaux and able to carry about 20 tons more cargo, but they had a draught of 28 inches as compared to 20 inches. The smaller, shallower-draught bateaux were ideally suited to turbulent rivers strewn with rapids but on the Montreal-Lachine route a proper canal with locks 16 feet wide by three feet deep was planned to take advantage of the superior carrying capacity of the Durham boats.

While planning proceeded on the Ottawa-Rideau communication, the Colonial Office created a Military Settling Department to oversee the settlement of discharged veterans in strategic areas of Upper Canada. Priority was given to the eastern counties closest to the proposed military lines of communication. British emigrants were also to be assisted to settle there to discourage the spread of American settlement. Under the direction of local military authorities, new townsites were laid out to the rear of the Rideau River with a wilderness buffer left between the river and the St. Lawrence front. It was expected that the military settlements would provide trained officers for militia units raised in the interior, and

the spread of settlement would foster a growing trade along the Rideau and Ottawa navigations. The military regarded towing bateaux through the rapids as a temporary measure until the increasing trade of the interior induced the provincial governments of Upper and Lower Canada to undertake, or at least contribute substantially toward, the cost of constructing proper canals. By that time, the military settlements would provide the labour force, draught animals, food and fodder required.

In the spring of 1817 the Ordnance's attempt to get work under way ground to a halt when the British Treasury refused to approve expenditures on a project not deemed of immediate importance. However, once again a threat from the United States persuaded the British to forge ahead. This time the threat was economic. In April 1817, work began on the American Erie Canal, raising the spectre of the Great Lakes trade flowing away from the St. Lawrence down the new canal to New York. Suddenly the government of Lower Canada expressed a willingness to undertake the construction of a canal from Montreal to Lachine. The imperial Treasury immediately agreed to contribute but the heavy impact of the postwar trade depression on the Canadas prevented further action by the colonial legislature until 1819, when a private company was authorized to raise the capital. At that time, the Duke of Richmond promised to purchase stock in the company in return for an agreement whereby military vessels would receive free passage through the canal in perpetuity. The company also decided, in concert with the military authorities, to construct the canal on an enlarged scale (locks 20 feet wide by 108 feet long with a five-foot depth of water) to permit the passage of gunboats which had been used during the war to convoy bateaux on the navigable stretches of the St. Lawrence.

Richmond also appropriated money to the construction of a canal at Grenville on the Long Sault Rapids up the Ottawa River. A survey conducted in 1818 indicated that of the four rapids on the proposed Ottawa bateaux route—the Ste. Anne's Rapids at the confluence of the Ottawa and St. Lawrence rivers, and the Carillon, Chute à Blondeau, and Long Sault Rapids farther up the Ottawa—only the Long Sault Rapids could not be readily improved to take fully laden bateaux. There a six-mile-long canal cut and locks were required to overcome a 60-foot change in elevation and the monies supplied by the Duke of Richmond were more than sufficient to cover the projected cost.

Meanwhile, efforts continued to get construction underway on the other fortifications and navigation routes required by the Canadian defence plan. In 1819 the new Master General of the Ordnance, the Duke of Wellington, received Treasury approval to build a magazine and barracks on St. Helen's Island at Montreal and the new fort at Isle aux Noix, and in the following year construction began on the new citadel at Quebec.

At Montreal, the legislature of Lower Canada took over construction of the Lachine Canal, which began in July 1821, and the Grenville Canal was enlarged to match the new gunboat scale of the Lachine project. The Ordnance, therefore, had cause to be pleased. Three of the four fortifications deemed necessary for the defence of the Canadas were under construction, two of the three canals were under way and the military settlement programme intended to facilitate the construction of the third canal had attracted 3500 men and their families into the Rideau River area. Only the Rideau navigation system and the Kingston fortifications were not yet undertaken.

At this point the provincial government of Upper Canada became interested in canal-building. Stimulated by the outburst of canal construction in Lower Canada and the American states, the Legislature of Upper Canada employed a civil engineer, Samuel Clowes, to survey and report on the potential cost and feasibility of constructing a number of canals in Upper Canada. After surveying the Rideau route, Clowes reported in September 1824 that there was insufficient water at the summit for a canal by the Irish Creek route but that an uninterrupted canal could be constructed on the Rideau Lakes route by connecting the Cataraqui and Rideau rivers. However, Clowes reported, it would require extensive canal cuts and more than 53 locks to overcome a total difference of elevation of 422 feet, and it would be a costly undertaking. The British government offered to help Upper Canada finance the canal project but the province, which had just begun the Welland Canal to circumvent Niagara Falls, preferred the existing St. Lawrence route and rejected the offer. A secure military communication in the Rideau interior would have to be constructed solely by the British government.

Financing the Rideau Project

There appears to be no difficulty whatever . . . .
Smyth Report
9 September 1825

In the spring of 1825 the Duke of Wellington despatched a Commission of Royal Engineers, under Sir James Carmichael Smyth, to examine the defences of British North America and report on the cost and feasibility of additional fortifications and an extensive canal system in Upper Canada. Wellington, in effect, had decided that the proposed interior water system from Montreal to Kingston should be extended through the Trent waterway with a network of canals connecting the Trent with Lake Erie, via the Ouse (Grand) River, and with Lake St. Clair, via the Thames River. The Smyth Commission reported in September 1825 that most, if not all, of the canals and fortifications required to implement Wellington's plan could be readily constructed, at a total cost of £1,141,218. But the commission recommended that the first phase of construction should concentrate on the critically important Quebec-Montreal-Kingston sector.

Based on Clowes's rough calculations, an uninterrupted gunboat canal, with locks on the Lachine Canal scale, could be constructed from the Ottawa River to Kingston via the Rideau Lakes route for £169,000. This figure would return to haunt the men responsible for the Rideau project. It was based on cursory preliminary estimates which experience of other construction projects showed to be completely unreliable. For example, the Cape Diamond citadel at Quebec would encounter a cost overrun of 300 per cent and on the Grenville Canal an extremely difficult excavation in hard compact rock had resulted in a projected overrun of 222 per cent.

The preliminary estimate of £169,000 did not take into account the heavy costs being incurred at the Grenville Canal or the much greater potential for higher costs on a more ambitious project carried out in a relatively unexplored wilderness.

Upon receipt of the Smyth report, the Ordnance planned to proceed with the works required at a projected expenditure of £100,000 per annum. With the Duke of Wellington firmly ensconced as Commander-in-Chief of the Army, as well as Master General of the Ordnance with a seat in cabinet, there was every reason to expect that the necessary monies might well be forthcoming. However, the government of the day, aghast at the sums involved, refused to submit such a costly colonial defence scheme to Parliament.

Only two new Canadian projects were sanctioned, the Rideau Canal and the Kingston fortifications, and each was to have a request for a mere £5000 inserted in the parliamentary estimate to cover expenditures in 1826. Despite the government's indifferent support, the Ordnance was determined to proceed as quickly as possible and in March 1826 two officers of the Corps of Royal Engineers, John By and Ross Wright, were appointed to superintend the projects.

Many of the problems associated with the completion of the Rideau Canal were created at the very beginning when it was decided to proceed in a manner totally unlike the usual Ordnance practice. The Kingston project offers a useful comparison. Colonel Wright was sent to Upper Canada to begin quarrying stone while he prepared a detailed plan and estimate. Work on the fortifications was not to start until the estimate was submitted to Parliament for approval. If Parliament refused to approve the expenditure required, Wright was to employ the quarried stone to repair the existing Kingston defences; if Parliament approved the expenditure, construction would proceed with a succession of annual parliamentary grants being voted, based on the estimate and the projected duration of the project.

Hiring practices were not spelled out but, traditionally, major Ordnance projects were carried on by employing soldier-artisans, such as companies of the Royal Staff Corps or Royal Sappers and Miners, and/or hiring civilian day workers at the start of each construction season to work under the direction of officers of the Royal Engineers. Once the amount of the annual parliamentary grant was expended in any given year, day workers were dismissed, the companies of soldier-artisans recalled to barracks, and work on the project suspended until the following year. In this manner Parliament maintained direct control over Ordnance expenditures.

On the other hand, a novel procedure was adopted for the Rideau Canal. It was to be constructed exclusively by contract on a system which would not be tied to the amount of the annual parliamentary grant. Construction of canals by contract was expected to increase the speed of the project and would result in substantial savings in overall costs. To realize the full advantages of the contract system, it was essential that contractors be free to begin work as early as possible in the spring without waiting for notification as to the amount of the annual grant. Contractors also had to be free to push the work on as quickly as possible over the duration of the project without fear of having it curtailed should they exceed the grant in any given year. Therefore the Rideau Canal was to be constructed on multi-year, open-ended contracts, to be let to the lowest bidder through the army Commissariat Department. Contractors would be paid as the work progressed at the agreed rate per cubic yard of rock and earth excavated, and per cubic foot of masonry laid.

Because such a system deprived the superintending engineer of control over his annual expenditures, the Commissariat, which was to furnish Colonel By with the monies he needed as construction proceeded, was instructed by the Ordnance to make payments from the military chest on receipt of proper vouchers, regardless of whether the total sum requested was greater or lesser than the amount of the parliamentary grant in any given year. The Commissariat in turn was to be reimbursed by the Colonial Office, on whose estimates the Rideau project was to be carried in Parliament.

It was assumed, of course, that if the annual grant was overspent in one year, the total expenditure nonetheless would even out by the close of the project. Parliament was to be deprived of its control over annual expenditures, but would still retain control over the sum ultimately expended if the new system functioned properly and, most importantly, if the estimate proved accurate. As a further compromise, the Ordnance was prepared to proceed with the Rideau Canal before a detailed estimate could be prepared and submitted to Parliament.

Following his appointment, Colonel By was dispatched to Lower Canada to make preliminary arrangements until Parliament voted the £5000 to cover Rideau expenditures in 1826. He was then to proceed to Upper Canada and begin construction, pushing it forward as quickly as possible, without waiting for the annual grant and while completing his plans and estimates. In other words, By could start building his canal before he had the money to do so.

On its own initiative the Ordnance, with the concurrence of the Colonial Office, had decided that the vote would constitute sufficient approval for the Rideau project to be carried on until such time as By's estimate was received. Parliament would be presented with a fait accompli. Once By's estimate was received, Parliament would either have to authorize the major expenditures it entailed, or cancel the project at a cost of writing off the monies already spent which might well be far in excess of the monies voted. However, these implications were as yet unperceived when By, accompanied by his wife and two daughters, left England in April 1826 to take up his new duties in Upper Canada.

Construction of the Rideau Canal

Getting the Project Under Way

> I feel confident the Rideau Canal will be completed . . . . in four years, although I have great doubts whether it can be performed for £ 169,000 . . . .
>
> *Colonel By*
> *6 December 1826*

While living in Montreal during the summer of 1826, Colonel By gathered information about canal construction and interviewed prospective overseers and clerks for appointment to his engineering staff. Finally, on September 4, he received word that Parliament had approved the £5000 Rideau appropriation for 1826. On-site preparations were to begin at once so that contractors might start their work as soon as possible in the new year without waiting for the parliamentary grant. These instructions, which for the most part merely recapitulated his earlier orders, fitted in well with By's eagerness to get on with the job.

If construction was to start in the spring of 1827, the establishment of a support system had to begin immediately, and survey work had to be completed to a point that the Commissariat Department could prepare major contracts for tender during the winter of 1826-27. No time was to be lost. The water levels Clowes recorded two years before had to be checked and the extent and ownership of the properties that would have to be purchased along the canal route had to be established. Further surveys would determine the precise location of canal structures while work proceeded on their planning and design. By departed from Montreal immediately and arrived on 21 September 1826 at Wright's Town (Hull) on the Ottawa River opposite the Rideau Falls.

Within days By selected a ravine in the rock cliff a mile above the Rideau Falls for the entrance to the canal and set his staff to work surveying the terrain. An opening ceremony was held on 26 September 1826 with the Governor-in-Chief, Lord Dalhousie, turning the first sod. After securing Dalhousie's permission to temporarily dispense with contract tendering, By let contracts on the spot for preliminary work including clearing the Entrance Valley, and constructing two wharves on the river, a number of log support buildings, a blacksmith's shop, and a carpenter's shop. Two town sites, Bytown and Lower Bytown, were surveyed on either side of the canal route and work began on a series of seven bridges across the islands at the Chaudière Falls to provide easy access to Wright's Town.

During November and December, a survey crew was kept busy in the interior taking levels and determining the precise location of the canal route. This followed By's general line from the head of the Entrance Valley, some 80 feet above the Ottawa River, across a slight depression named Dows Great Swamp, and through the highlands beyond to join the Rideau River at the 100-foot level above

the Hog's Back Rapids some six and a half miles inland. From that point By planned to follow Clowes's line along the river systems and, if all went well, he hoped to have up to 6000 men employed on all sections of the route during the 1827 season.

Plans were prepared for additional stone buildings needed at Bytown: a barracks for a detachment to guard the gunpowder and military chest, a hospital, an officers' quarters, and two large storehouses comprising a Royal Engineers' office and a Commissariat office to house the Ordnance paymaster and stores. These contracts were advertised for tender in February with the work to be completed by the following June. Further contracts were advertised in Montreal and New York newspapers for the excavation and masonry work required on the first section of the canal, from the Entrance Valley to the Hog's Back inclusive, with the contracts to be awarded on May 4, 1827. After again securing permission from Dalhousie to enter into contracts on the spot if acceptable bids were received for work deemed to be immediately necessary, By travelled the canal route by canoe in May 1827 with experienced contractors wishing to undertake work on the project.

The Rideau project was plagued by difficulties imposed by its isolation and a lack of suitable building materials. Detailed surveys proceeded much more slowly than anticipated in the dense swamps and on the heavily forested banks of the rivers. Technical difficulties were compounded by the suffering inflicted by swarms of mosquitoes and black flies, dysentery and malaria. Bids for work on the interior locksites proved to be exorbitantly high, reflecting the absence of either a road or a navigable waterway by which tools, materials, and supplies could be transported to the site. Lastly, By was frustrated by the lack of stone suitable for quarrying near many of the Cataraqui River locksites. He was forced to contract settlers to search for lime and sand, locate and open stone quarries, clear locksites, and cut roads through the forest before he could put the major excavation and masonry work out for contract.

Nevertheless, during the 1827 season preliminary work was under way on all but one of the Cataraqui locksites as well as a number of sites on the Rideau River. Once a road was opened connecting Richmond Landing with the Entrance Valley and the Entrance Valley with the locksites as far up as Long Island, excavation and masonry work on the first 14 miles of canal was let at moderate rates. When work was suspended at the end of October, excavation was well under way on the first section of canal, three locks were under construction in the Entrance Valley, and the initial survey and lock layout plans were advanced sufficiently to enable contracts to be prepared for letting early in the new year. Construction would begin on all of the remaining locksites and canal cuts in the spring of 1828.

Colonel By's Master Plan

I have no other motive in thus strongly recommending the large lock, but the good of my Country.

Colonel By
23 January 1828

By had always doubted the preliminary estimate of £169,000 that the Ordnance had come to accept. He knew that the Lachine Canal, a relatively shallow cut eight miles long with seven locks overcoming an elevation of only 44 feet, had cost over £100,000, and it was built close to men, materials and provisions. In contrast the Rideau would cross more than 120 miles of virtual wilderness where, according to Clowes's report, some 25 miles of canal cuts and up to 50 locks would be needed to overcome a total difference of elevation of 422 feet.

So By was not surprised when he calculated that it would cost £474,844 to construct the Rideau Canal with 20-by-108-foot gunboat locks. However, this was not the only shock By had in store for the Ordnance. He wanted to build a canal able to handle the largest lake steamboats, an inland transport system on a scale far beyond anything then in existence.

By's ambitious plan began to take shape soon after his arrival in Montreal. His reasons were both military and commercial and his vision encompassed more than just the Rideau system. He argued that the Canadas could best be defended by constructing an uninterrupted steamboat route connecting the Great Lakes with the St. Lawrence River by way of the Welland, Rideau, Ottawa and Lachine canals. It would give Great Britain control over the trade of the fertile hinterlands of the Great Lakes by drawing all the exports of the region down the St. Lawrence and it would open new markets for British manufactured goods. Trade could be confined to Canadian shipping and the steamboats readily armed in wartime. As of 1826 there were a dozen steamboats operating on the major lakes and rivers that would comprise the proposed navigation, and these vessels, in By's estimation, were capable of transporting an army of 10,000 men. As trade expanded, the number of steamboats would multiply at no additional expense to the British government, and British forces could be marshalled in strength at any given point on the frontier with a rapidity of movement the Americans could not match. Consequently, control of the lakes could be maintained and a perfect security provided against American attack.

This was ultimately the most economical way of defending the Canadas. It required only the building of several new, relatively short canals and the enlarging of the canals already constructed or about to be constructed to enable the largest of the lake steamboats — vessels approximately 130 feet long by 48 feet wide with an eight-foot draught fully loaded — to pass from the ocean to the Great Lakes. By stated he could build the whole system, with locks 50 feet by 150 feet on a ten-foot-deep waterway, in four or five years at a total cost of about £1,200,000.

Large locks would be able to accommodate the timber trade, then the mainstay of the Canadian export economy, as well as steamboats hauling passengers and freight, and By had been assured by a number of Montreal forwarders that moderate tolls would yield, within a decade, as much as 20 per cent per annum on the projected cost.

This was Colonel By's master plan and the Ordnance Department agreed that it had immense commercial and military advantages. Nonetheless the Ordnance turned his recommendation down on the grounds that steamboats could not operate on canals, and towing them through such an extensive canal system would provide no advantage over towing barges through the smaller scale of canal. Moreover, the Ordnance suspected that its construction would entail far greater expenditures.

Leaving aside the question of cost, which militated against By's proposal, there was much to be said in favour of the Ordnance's decision based on the situation as it was perceived from England. Despite their unquestioned commercial success on the major rivers of the British Isles and North America, steamboats were not used on canals. In every British experiment, the wash of paddle wheels had destroyed the canal banks. The only effective remedies were to protect the clay banks with walling or paving, both prohibitively expensive, or to ban steamboats from canals, as was generally done in Britain.

Moreover, the scale of canal By proposed to build was unprecedented. British canals varied in size but generally had either broad locks, roughly 13 feet wide by 65 feet long, or narrow locks, 7½ feet wide by 70 feet long, and both had proved more than adequate to meet the demands of British trade. In North America the Erie Canal was four feet deep with broad locks 15 feet wide by 90 feet long. The Lachine Canal was somewhat larger again with locks 20 feet by 108 feet.

The only British or North American canal on anywhere near the scale By proposed was the 60-mile-long Caledonian Ship Canal which bisected Scotland. There it had taken 19 years and £905,250 to construct 21½ miles of canal cuts and 29 masonry locks, 40 feet by 170 feet with 15 feet of water on the sills. The Ordnance understandably was not interested in becoming involved in constructing comparatively large locks (50 feet by 150 feet) on a much more extensive system.

Refusing to abandon his plan entirely, in the fall of 1827 By met Ordnance objections by reducing the scale of his proposal. He argued that if the Rideau system alone was constructed with large locks of only five-foot depth, instead of ten, the major commercial and military advantages of a through steamboat navigation would still be realized. Operating steamboats would pose no problems: almost 100 miles of the 123-mile-long Rideau waterway would consist of either broad lakes or wide rivers, the banks of which were scoured each spring by floods ranging as high as 15 feet above the mean level of the river, and the other rivers between Quebec and the Rideau were similarly immune to injury from the wash of paddle wheels. Moreover, the Rideau canal cuts would be made chiefly through rock.

Steamboats were too large for the Lachine or Ottawa canals, but they could be stationed on the long navigable stretches of the St. Lawrence and Ottawa rivers to tow Durham boats which then could be towed by horse or oxen through the intervening canals without any need for transhipment. At the head of the Grenville Canal, cargoes could be transhipped into the large lake steamboats which, if not fully loaded, would be capable of passing through the large, five-foot-deep locks on the Rideau Canal to Lake Ontario and beyond at great savings in time and transport costs.

In 1815 it had cost £4.10 per ton to move military supplies and as much as £200 to transport a 24-pounder cannon weighing 53 hundredweight from Quebec to Kingston on the laborious bateaux journey up the St. Lawrence. If the Rideau was constructed to handle steamboats, By pointed out, the 447 miles from Quebec to Kingston via the Ottawa and Rideau could be covered in less than three and a half days of steaming time, and the cost of transport reduced substantially to £1.3 per ton for stores and £5 per 24-pounder.

The multiplicity of Rideau locksites, 22 in all, ruled out stationing steamboats on the navigable stretches between the locks. If the locks were not large enough for steamboats to circulate through the Rideau system, By argued, vessels would have to rely on oar or sail as towpaths were impractical on 70 miles of the canal where the banks consisted of either high rocky cliffs or low-lying flood plains and swamps. In the face of contrary winds and the absence of towpaths, gunboats and transport vessels could well be subject to long delays that would not affect steamboats.

Furthermore, the speed and ease of transport provided by steamboats on the Rideau Canal would enable the Kingston dockyard, as well as the Ordnance and naval depots, to be removed to Bytown from their relatively exposed positions on the frontier at Kingston. Frigates could be constructed in complete security on the Ottawa River at Bytown and towed by steamboat through the Rideau Canal to Kingston to be ballasted and armed for service on Lake Ontario.

Yet another advantage of the large locks of five-foot depth was that they could take the rafts, or cribs, of squared timber that were floated down to Quebec for export, and the 130-foot-long spars destined for the Royal Navy. The timber trade could continue to function on the Ottawa and St. Lawrence irrespective of their small canal locks; those locks were constructed in canal cuts bypassing the rapids, the rivers being left unimpeded. On the Rideau system, high dams would block the rivers and if timber cribs and spars could not pass through the locks, the cribs would have to be taken apart and, like the spars, dragged overland at each of the 22 locksites in turn, by no means a minor consideration.

Lastly, By pointed out that the cost of constructing the Rideau Canal with larger locks was not much greater than for gunboat locks of the same depth. The surveying, clearing and purchasing of the land, the forming of temporary coffer dams, the construction of the dams and embankments, and even the thickness of the lock masonry and the depth of the excavations would remain unaffected by the change in lock dimensions. Extra masonry would be required for the larger locks, and the width of the excavations would have to be increased, but the latter increase was not as substantial as would have been the case on a conventional canal project where rapids were bypassed or rivers avoided entirely by means of long canal cuts. On the Rideau Canal, By planned to construct high dams to flood the rapids and the raising of the waters would considerably reduce the length of the cuts. By estimated that the five-foot-deep large-lock system would cost only £527,844, about £50,000 more than he had estimated for the smaller scale system.

By's Plan is Vindicated

It appears to me that Lieut. Colonel By has lost sight entirely of the Plan and Estimates for the Work . . . .

Duke of Wellington
29 December 1827

By's November plans and estimate were not well received when they arrived in London in December 1827. The Board of Ordnance was severely jolted, particularly as it had, in the spring of 1827, forwarded the £169,000 preliminary estimate for submission to Parliament. Parliament had subsequently not only approved the Rideau project on the basis of the preliminary estimate, but also voted £41,000 to cover expenditures in 1827 with the intention of voting similar sums over each of the three remaining years. Now, according to By, the project would cost three times more than expected.

A committee of senior officers of the Royal Engineers, the Bryce Committee, was appointed to examine By's plans and estimate. The inquiry soon took on a different complexion when Wellington called for a more wide-ranging inquiry on the grounds that By had totally departed from the original plan without informing the Ordnance or obtaining their consent. It was possible, he allowed, that By was right in discarding Clowes's plan, but that remained to be determined. By's plans had also to be examined, particularly his scheme of constructing high dams to flood the rapids.

Once the engineering committee determined which plan was the more practicable and least costly, a second committee should be sent to Upper Canada. If By's plan were accepted, the second committee should also investigate the cost and advantages of increasing the lock size. In the meantime, Wellington recommended limiting Rideau expenditures for 1828 to £40,000 and instructing By to enter into no new contracts until government approval was obtained.

Early in January 1828, a new government, in which Wellington served as Prime Minister and First Lord of the Treasury, took office and henceforth the actions of the Ordnance were strictly in keeping with his recommendations. Orders were despatched to By to suspend all work not demanding immediate execution, and to persuade the contractors to suspend the contracts already in force. The Bryce Committee began an examination of By's and Clowes's plans and estimates, while Lieutenant General Sir James Kempt, the Lieutenant Governor of Nova Scotia, was ordered to the Rideau in the spring to serve as president of a second engineering committee to be sent out from London.

The Bryce Committee report, submitted to the Ordnance on January 23, 1828, completely exonerated By. The committee noted that By had indeed deviated in a number of places from Clowes's route and he had substituted high dams to flood the rapids in place of Clowes's canal cuts around the rapids and fewer low dams. Nonetheless, they concluded that in every instance, By's changes would mean substantial savings, and the high dams, although admittedly of an uncommon, even extreme, height, appeared feasible and economical compared to the cost of the rock cutting required for lengthier canal cuts. Overall, the committee found By's estimate and surveys to have been framed with great care and accuracy, and they recommended only minor alterations.

The Bryce Committee was not surprised that By's estimate exceeded Clowes's preliminary estimate which was at best a rough calculation of what each proposed structure or cutting would cost. Clowes had not prepared plans for any of the structures, nor taken sections or borings. Moreover, Clowes had not allowed for contingencies, whereas By had included the customary one-tenth. Although the committee commended Clowes's skill and industry, they concluded that his report was intended more to show the practicability of a canal rather than accurate costs. Consequently, they were convinced that By had not lost sight of the original plan and estimate.

On the important question of whether the Rideau Canal should be built with the 20-foot-wide gunboat locks as originally planned or constructed with the 50-foot-wide steamboat locks By advocated, the committee expressed an ambivalent attitude based on an evident reluctance to approve further heavy expenditures. They saw no immediate advantage in constructing large steamboat locks solely on the Rideau system, but were of the opinion that great military advantages would accrue if the provinces had the financial resources in future to construct a large-lock system from Quebec to Lake Ontario.

The Board of Ordnance approved the Bryce Committee report and forwarded it to the Colonial Office on January 26, 1828, but two major questions remained to be resolved: the size of lock and the expenditure for 1828. These decisions were to be made by the Colonial Office, which was carrying the Rideau estimates in Parliament.

Following a perusal of the Bryce Committee report, By's reports and the Smyth Commission report of 1825, the Colonial Secretary, William Huskisson, informed the Ordnance in March 1828 that the large-lock question would be decided by the Kempt Committee. If the committee should agree with By that it would cost £527,844, they were to authorize him to construct larger locks or locks of any intermediate size that appeared most expedient. Huskisson proposed to postpone any new demands on Parliament pending the receipt of the Kempt Committee report, and to request £41,000 from Parliament for 1828 in keeping with the appropriation voted the previous year and Wellington's views. However, it soon became apparent that major expenditures could no longer be deferred or avoided.

On the distant Upper Canadian frontier By unwittingly was frustrating attempts by the Colonial Office to move slowly. The work restraint order had not reached him in time and he was busily contracting work for the 1828 season. In January 1828, By reported that £28,614.7.2 had been spent on existing contracts since November 1827, in addition to the £32,621.13.5 total expenditure reported for the Rideau project as of November 1st. All of the remaining work would be contracted out by February 2, 1828. On receipt of By's report, it was evident that the contracts were already let and any attempt to void these arrangements would probably entail onerous concessions by the government as well as the loss of the monies spent to date. On the other hand, if the contracts remained in force, the £41,000 Huskisson planned to request from Parliament would be insufficient. However, this posed no difficulty for the Colonial Secretary. He had come to terms with the revised Rideau Canal estimate, and was able to take this latest development in stride.

The Bryce Committee report had proved to Huskisson's satisfaction that a much greater outlay would be required to construct the Rideau Canal than previously estimated, and he now saw clearly that a large expenditure was required in the present year no matter what action the government might take. To his mind, the blame rested directly on the inadequacy of the Clowes estimate, although he regretted that By should have felt himself at liberty to conclude contracts involving a far greater expenditure of public money than initially anticipated.

Huskisson decided to request £120,000 from Parliament in 1828. This would more than meet By's contract obligations to the close of the year. In succeeding years, even larger sums would no doubt be required, but those amounts could be left, as planned, until the Kempt report was received. The Ordnance drew up detailed instructions for the Kempt Committee in keeping with Huskisson's views, and forwarded them to the Rideau with two officers who were to serve on the committee.

During the winter of 1827-28, By's Rideau estimate was but one of a series of reports the Ordnance received from the Royal Engineers who had been despatched in 1826-27 to prepare detailed plans and estimates for the works recommended by the Smyth Commission. Almost all of the estimates exceeded the preliminary estimates formed by the Smyth Commission, and the sum required to construct the Canadian defence scheme rose from £1,686,944 to £2,335,544. To make the cost of the scheme more palatable to Parliament, the Ordnance planned to request, during the summer of 1828, support only for works of immediate importance. The Rideau project required £120,000, the Ottawa canals £15,000, and appropriations were needed for the Fort Lennox and Quebec citadel projects. In addition the Ordnance planned to request approval to start the Kingston fortifications, the Montreal citadel project, defensive works on the southern approach to Montreal at St. Helen's, Châteauguay and St. Jean, and the Halifax citadel. The importance of the Rideau Canal in Wellington's scheme is evident in the fact that with Huskisson's acceptance of the increase in the Rideau estimate to a potential £527,844, the canal came to represent by far the largest single expenditure in British North America contemplated by the imperial government. By's arguments had all but carried the day in London.

Another Committee Meets

> The increase of the estimate is certainly enormous but those who framed the original one may be the Persons to blame and not Colonel By.
>
> *Sir James Kempt*
> *5 March 1828*

Ironically, By was left in the dark about developments in London. On the Rideau all he received was the work restraint order and he was left struggling to comply with it.

The spring of 1828 was especially trying. If large locks were to be constructed with a minimum loss of work and materials, a decision had to arrive before the start of the work season, and time was rapidly running out. He had expected the Ordnance's decision long since; the delay was greater than the usual eight- to nine-week time lag in communications between London and the Rideau. Indeed, he was just receiving the Ordnance's initial, shocked reaction to his estimate. The work restraint order arrived on March 10th, informing him that £41,000 would probably be appropriated for 1828, and that he was to limit expenditures accordingly. This placed By in the embarrassing position of trying his utmost to comply with these instructions while at the same time being fully aware, as he hastened to write to his superiors, of the impossibility of doing so.

By had not been idle on the Rideau. He had managed to let, on two-year contracts at moderate rates, all of the remaining excavation and masonry work. Now, to cut down on his expenditures, By immediately discharged the sawyers, smiths, carpenters, labourers and squad masters employed directly by the Rideau engineering department, and let it be known that the government wished to proceed more slowly, especially as the lock size had yet to be determined.

By requested the contractors to accept an extension of their contracts for at least a year, and tried to discourage them from pressing their work in the present year. However, the contractors were convinced that the more rapidly the works were completed the greater their profits would be. They threatened legal action if their work was impeded in any way. By was placed in a distressing situation, made all the more so as he had previously encouraged the contractors to work with the utmost vigour, and a recent tour of inspection had confirmed that all the contractors were busy laying in provisions, forage and tools, and collecting men for the coming work season.

As the weeks passed into months and still no word was received from the Ordnance, the situation on the Rideau became increasingly difficult. Despite his best efforts, By could not exercise any real control over the expenditures rapidly depleting his allotted funds. Although the contractors had agreed to a one-year extension of their contracts, they steadfastly refused to bind themselves to any limitation on their rate of progress. Elsewhere, all of By's efforts resulted in trifling savings.

Moreover, he soon confessed to Colonel Durnford, the Commanding Royal Engineer for the Canadas, that he had acted too hastily in dismissing his day workers. These men provided the templates and profiles required by the contractors to guide their work, and he feared that if they were not re-employed, the contractors would sue for damages for any resultant delays. Compared to the damages that might be awarded, the wages of the men were insignificant, and By received Durnford's support for his decision to take them back on the payroll. As of May 1828, By reported that at the rate the work was progressing, he would find it difficult to confine his expenditures to £100,000 in 1828, let alone £41,000.

Nevertheless, By was confident that additional monies would be forthcoming from the Ordnance and was eager to resume the work. During the spring of 1828, setbacks had been experienced at only two sites: at the Hog's Back, where sudden floods in February and again in April caused extensive damage to the dam under construction there; and at the Chaudière crossing, where the last and largest of the seven bridges under construction collapsed. Once he returned from his now-customary spring tour of inspection, By intended to begin rebuilding the destroyed structures.

Indeed, his major vexation was contractors who complained incessantly of being held up by the suspension of further masonry work pending the resolution of the lock size. Only so much preliminary work could be done, and with the lock masonry work in abeyance and the allotted funds approaching exhaustion, work ground almost to a halt during May.

The only communication By received from the Ordnance was an inquiry as to whether he intended to carry his establishment on his contingency allowance. On June 10th By wrote to the Ordnance explaining that Dalhousie had assured him that the cost of the Rideau establishment would be carried on the army Extraordinaries, as was the case with the Ottawa Canals establishment, and consequently the Rideau estimate covered only the actual cost of the canal. Otherwise the Rideau estimate would have to be increased.

It was already evident that the bedrock in several of the lockpit excavations was not sufficiently sound to serve as a lock floor, requiring the building of more masonry lock floors than anticipated, and the outbreak of malaria at several locksites had necessitated clearing the forest from those sites to ensure a better circulation of air for the benefit of the workers' health. Moreover, the heavy dam construction work alone was subject to flood damages which the ten-per-cent contingency allowance would scarcely cover. Simply to meet the cost of the establishment over the course of the project through 1831, the estimate would have to be increased by over £60,000.

The Kempt Committee arrived at Kingston on June 15, 1828, where they were met by Colonel By. Kempt immediately began a methodical investigation. The committee was somewhat surprised at the magnitude of the project, yet highly pleased by the quantity of work that had been accomplished and the way in which the project was organized. But they must have been taken aback when By submitted to them a substantially revised estimate.

Over £60,000 would have to be added to the estimate to cover the cost of the military and civilian establishment. Further, it had proved impossible to route the canal to avoid destroying several saw and grist mills, and changing the canal configuration at Kingston Mills would result in the drowning of over 1300 acres of private wastelands. The estimate would have to include funds to buy out the mill owners and to compensate landowners, bringing the Rideau estimate for the gunboat locks to £544,676, and for a steamboat system of five-foot depth to £597,676. Both estimates were greater than the maximum expenditure the Colonial Office had in view when Huskisson authorized the Kempt Committee to decide the scale of the Rideau locks.

On June 28, 1828, the Kempt Committee completed their report. The Rideau navigation as By planned it was practicable and, with the high dams, would have sufficient water to operate effectively in the driest of seasons. By deserved commendation as his zealous efforts had helped to secure low tenders for the work, and, in keeping with the spirit of his instructions, he had inspired a degree of exertion in his work force that few individuals could have accomplished. The work being as far advanced as it was, the committee saw no alternative but to let construction continue until the government decided otherwise. For their part they feared that any suspension of the work might result in the government being sued for breach of contract. By was ordered to proceed, but limit his expenditures for 1828 to £105,000, in keeping with the sum to be requested from Parliament.

In deciding the lock size question, the primary consideration of the committee was to secure a dependable means of propulsion for military transport vessels. The construction of the Rideau on a scale to take steamboats, either as towboats or cargo vessels, was imperative. Consideration was given to constructing the large lock on a seven-foot-deep navigation, but surveys indicated that the banks were not high enough to allow the water to be raised that much and deepening the canal beyond five feet would be prohibitively expensive. Constructing large locks without a proportionately deep canal was adjudged to be of no particular advantage.

Accordingly, the committee decided the Rideau Canal should be five feet deep and have locks sufficiently large to take the smallest of the steam towboats operating on the open waters of the Ottawa River. These sidewheelers were 108 feet long by 30 feet wide across their paddleboxes, with four-foot draughts and it was calculated that their 32-horsepower engines could easily tow two fully laden Durham boats at a speed of four to five miles per hour in quiet water. Moreover, the committee noted, there were more than enough Durham boats currently in use on the St. Lawrence to provide ample transport for military and naval stores in the event of war, and the Durham boats would be able to pass through the whole of the navigation system from Montreal to Kingston without transhipping their cargoes.

In addition to several recommendations setting forth how the Rideau accounts were to be kept and the work supervised, the committee instructed By to prepare an estimate for the new scale of canal and to take steps to provide for its defence. Henceforth, lockmasters' houses were to be built as defensible guardhouses and situated so as to provide a protective fire for the locks and dams. By was also to determine where major military works might best be built for the defence of the canal and arrange for the purchase or reservation of the land required. In particular, he was directed to make an accurate survey of the Bytown area and reserve sufficient land for the eventual construction of a 5000-man fortified depot.

By immediately prepared a plan for the new scale of lock, which was to be 33 feet wide by 134 feet long instead of the 50 feet by 150 feet he had wanted. The revised estimate of £576,757 included the cost of the Rideau establishment as well as the damages to be paid to mill and land owners whose properties would be innundated. It did not include the cost of constructing military works and bridges along the canal or the purchase of the land needed for military purposes as these needs had not yet been determined. By also informed the Kempt Committee, as later, in 1829, he was to inform the Ordnance, that the estimate was the probable sum required, not an absolute figure. There were too many unforeseeable contingencies to which such a large project was subject.

By maintained that the best he could do was to record separately in his progress reports the expenditure made on each work, detailing where and from what cause any excess or saving on the estimate arose. The committee agreed to this procedure, but By's statement that the ten-per-cent contingency allowance might well not be enough was passed over in their report. The committee also took no action to relieve By of any of his contracts to assist him to keep his expenditures below the limit imposed for 1828, and in subsequent years, following Parliament's acceptance of the new Rideau estimate, the Ordnance did not rescind By's original instructions to drive the work forward without regard to the amount of the annual parliamentary grant.

Despite misgivings based on his lack of control over expenditures with the open-ended contracts remaining in force, By was nonetheless highly pleased with the Kempt Committee report. The new scale of lock would accommodate spars, timber cribs, and small river steamboats, thereby providing the cheapness and speed of transport necessary to realize the military and commercial potential that he envisaged for the Rideau. The new locks would not take frigates so the Kingston dockyard could not be moved to the security of the Ottawa River at Bytown, but this did not affect other aspects of By's strategy of a mobile defence. Large lake steamboats were likewise excluded from the Rideau Canal, but this meant merely that troops and supplies would have to be transferred into the lake steamboats at Kingston rather than at Grenville. The speed of transit would not be affected.

Triumph and Tribulation

Immediate steps [must be taken] for removing Colonel By . . . . and for placing some competent person in charge of those works . . . .

Treasury Lords
25 May 1832

They are very magnificent works, and done in a most substantial manner.

Colonel Durnford
15 June 1832

As soon as the Kempt Committee handed down its instructions, By left for Bytown, laying out the new scale of lock for the contractors as he passed each locksite. As of the first of August 1828, work was again under way on all of the locksites and at Bytown the contractor was beginning to lay the floor of the first lock to be constructed on the new scale. At the end of that year By was able to report that an astonishing quantity of work had been accomplished, the project was on schedule, and expenditures had fallen just short of the £105,000 limit. Although By's expenditures to the close of 1829 were well in excess of what Parliament had voted to date, the Ordnance was not overly concerned. The work was proceeding rapidly, and a potential excess in expenditure over the annual grant in any given year had always been anticipated. But the worst was yet to come as costs continued to mount and a hostile government took steps to rein in the project.

On March 15, 1830, By forwarded a detailed supplementary estimate to the Ordnance covering the cost of additional works required on the canal. It revealed a potential cost overrun of £30,000 on the items in the June 1828 estimate, and that an additional £83,714 would be required to construct a waste weir at each locksite. The original concept of having overflow dams perform a dual function of maintaining water levels and carrying off surplus water had proved impractical in view of the damage inflicted during the spring floods on the several low dams already constructed. Furthermore, carrying out the defence measures recommended by the Kempt Committee would bring the total estimate to £762,679.

Upon receipt of By's March 1830 estimate, the Ordnance decided to postpone the military works, but accepted the necessity of the waste weirs and the cost overrun, which was not all that unexpected in view of the large sums being spent prosecuting works in a wilderness. In August the Treasury was informed of the new estimate of £693,449 and Parliament subsequently accepted it. However, in November 1830 a Reform government opposed to large-scale colonial defence expenditures succeeded Wellington's government, and in March 1831, when the 1831 Rideau grant was put before Parliament, the Chancellor of the Exchequer asked the House to appoint a select committee to decide whether the project should be abandoned to save further expense.

The select committee report of April 22, 1831, was severely critical of the Ordnance for the manner in which the Rideau project was undertaken. It rebuked the Ordnance for authorizing open-ended contracts and for neglecting to inform Parliament of the adoption of such an irregular and improper practice. The contract system, the committee noted, made it impossible for By to control his annual expenditures and it was therefore understandable that they might well overrun the annual grant. The committee recommended that parliamentary control over colonial construction projects be restored by requiring that all estimates be submitted for approval before construction began and that all contracts be subject to the limits of the annual parliamentary grant, except in circumstances authorized by Treasury.

The Treasury agreed with the committee and imposed new regulations on July 8, 1831. Once its control over expenditures was clearly defined, Parliament voted

£256,000 to cover By's expenditures to the scheduled close of the Rideau project in August 1831, bringing its total vote to £692,666, just short of the supplementary estimate it had approved the previous year. Although there was good reason to expect that the Rideau contracts might well necessitate expenditures in excess of the 1831 grant, the Ordnance did not inform the Treasury of that possibility nor seek approval to exceed the grant, if required, to finish the canal. Likewise, no new orders were forwarded to By.

Earlier, in May 1831, Sir James Kempt, newly appointed Master General of the Ordnance, had instructed By not to undertake any new work unless it were deemed of pressing importance and necessary to the completion of the canal and its defence — a meaningless admonition. Thereafter, probably in recognition of By's lack of control over his expenditures under the existing contracts and the imminent completion date for the project, no effort was made to inform By of either the July 1831 financial regulations or the amount of the 1831 grant. By was left, in ignorance of developments in London, to struggle as best he could to keep expenditures within the March 1830 estimate.

The problems and difficulties that had plagued the Rideau project from its beginning became steadily worse as construction continued at the Cataraqui River locksites, playing havoc with By's estimate and the progress of the work. A recurrence of malaria brought work there to a standstill each year during August and September, forcing expensive winter excavation work. Costs were further inflated by unexpectedly difficult rock excavation. Several contractors died of malaria and others defaulted on their contracts when it became apparent their contract rate was insufficient to recover their costs. By was forced to pay high wages to day workers to encourage them to report to the fever-ridden sites, or had to contract out the work again at higher rates, in several instances at double the original price.

Masonry prices also were increased to compensate contractors at locksites where sound building stone was not found nearby. Surveying and levelling difficulties increased immeasurably in the swamps and bogs of the Cataraqui River system, and all along the canal, landowners pressed unreasonable claims for damages and demanded compensation for expropriated properties.

On January 8, 1831, By forwarded a detailed report on his expenditures to the close of 1830 to Colonel Durnford at Quebec in keeping with Ordnance instructions that Durnford should verify the necessity of all future expenditures. By's report stated that £575,551 had been spent on the Rideau to the close of 1830, and the canal was proceeding on schedule within the March 1830 estimate. However, by July 1831, By estimated that the final cost of the canal would be £719,074. In effect, the March 1830 estimate would be exceeded by £25,625 if By's projection proved accurate.

Although the Ordnance received By's July 1831 estimate in September, no action was taken. The Ordnance had long since been put on the defensive by the growing hostility of Parliament and the Treasury to colonial defence expenditures. From the very inception of Wellington's scheme of defence, successive governments refused to submit it to Parliament. Piecemeal approval was obtained for a number of works until in 1828 Wellington insisted that his government submit the whole scheme to Parliament and request monies to proceed with six of the most important works. All six were rejected. Ultimately a compromise was reached but the fall of Wellington's government in November 1830 not only deprived the Ordnance Department of one of its strongest proponents, it brought to power a government that questioned the very principle of spending monies on colonial defence projects.

When By's projected cost overrun arrived in London, the Ordnance was preoccupied with working out a compromise agreement with the Treasury involving a slight increase in the Kingston fortifications estimate, and could ill-afford to anger the Treasury. Finally, in January 1832, the Treasury agreed to let work proceed on Fort Henry, the first of a series of six redoubts needed for the defence of the southern entrance of the Rideau Canal, and the dockyard at Kingston, with the stipulation that the remaining works were to be constructed one at a time, if approved by Parliament, on separate estimates.

On February 3, By's July 1831 estimate for the Rideau project was forwarded to the Treasury, and the Ordnance henceforth lost control of events. All of its past errors in judgment in launching the Rideau project rebounded to plague the Ordnance and By. The Treasury issued a stern rebuke to the Ordnance for the delay in forwarding By's latest report, and warned that the July 1831 regulations limited expenditures on Ordnance projects to the parliamentary grant in any given year.

At the close of 1831, By found that to finish the project would bring the total cost to £776,024. His report arrived at the Ordnance in May and was, this time, immediately forwarded to the Treasury. For the Lords of the Treasury, it was the last straw. They had seen the Rideau estimate escalate from £169,000 in 1827 to £693,449 in 1830. Now they were told the final estimate was even higher and the project would have to be extended into 1832.

What particularly incensed the Treasury was that By's expenditures to the end of 1831 were £22,000 in excess of the parliamentary grant for that year in apparent defiance of the new financial regulations, and By was obviously in the process of spending over £83,000 beyond the total amount Parliament had voted. On May 25, 1832, the Ordnance was instructed to recall By to explain his actions, and replace him with an officer under strict orders not to exceed the parliamentary grant to be voted for the coming year. The Ordnance had no choice but to comply with the Treasury directive and on June 1, 1832, By was called home.

Ironically, on the very day the Treasury directive demanded By's recall, he was celebrating the completion of the Rideau Canal. The official opening took place on May 24-29, when the By family, accompanied by various dignitaries, passed through the canal from Kingston to Bytown on the steamboat *Pumper*. Thereafter, By supervised various minor repairs and the setting up of an establishment to operate the canal. In August 1832 he received the order to return to England. He placed Captain Bolton of the Royal Engineers in charge of the canal, and went to Quebec to await the forwarding of papers required to prepare his last progress report on the Rideau expenditures. On October 23, 1832, By sailed for England, still unaware that he had been censured.

In Defence of By

I . . . . feel dreadfully ill-used.

Colonel By
23 January 1833

When By came home he found himself the object of not one but two inquiries. Before he had even left Canada a select parliamentary committee, the second to examine the Rideau project, expressed surprise that By had spent more than the estimate approved by Parliament and the annual grant for 1831, in contravention of the July 1831 regulations. In its report of June 29, 1832, the committee recommended that no further sums be allotted for Canadian canal projects beyond completing the canals already under way on the Ottawa. Further action was left to the Treasury inquiry which was to follow.

By himself was never called to testify before this formal inquiry. He submitted to Treasury the final cost for the canal project to August 31, 1832. This figure, £777,146.2.0, included property damage settlements and land purchases completed to that date, the building of several blockhouses and bridges, payment of the contractors, and repairs where embankments had settled when the water was raised in the canal. By calculated that perhaps an additional £20,000 would yet be required to complete payments for the inundated wastelands. The Rideau Canal Act of February 1827 had authorized the expropriation of lands required for the construction of the canal, but specified that disputes over purchase prices were to be determined by arbitration following the completion of the canal. Most of these disputes were settled by January 1834, raising the cost of the Rideau Canal to £822,804.

The Lords of the Treasury examined all By's expenditures, but directed their angry inquiries and accusations at the Ordnance. The Treasury was extremely hostile toward the Ordnance and By personally, yet was unable to sustain

any charges against him for either improper conduct or extravagant expenditures, and with good reason. From 1828 onwards, By had submitted detailed progress reports setting forth the original estimate for the works at each site, an itemized account of the monies spent to date, the amount required to complete the work, and a statement explaining where and why an excess or savings had been incurred. Indeed, his progress reports were far in advance of the general practice of the time.

Moreover, in 1828 the Bryce Committee had scrutinized By's plans and projected expenditures, and the Kempt Committee had investigated By's work and expenditures on the spot. Thereafter, Colonel Durnford had made periodic tours of the Rideau and verified all of By's accounts. Two select committees of the House of Commons had examined the Rideau accounts and, while highly critical of the Ordnance, made no criticism of By's conduct or expenditures. Nonetheless, as By complained to the Ordnance, the ministers were not reading his reports and appeared determined to hold him personally responsible for the heavy expenditures. They did not realize that the series of estimates submitted to Parliament were for different scales of canal or included items not in the original estimate, and they appeared to assume that he had expended monies without authority to do so.

Unfortunately for By, the Rideau project was completed during a time of political turmoil in Britain when events surrounding the Reform Bill of 1832 kept Parliament in a constant state of upheaval. In such a charged political atmosphere, what actually transpired on the Rideau was of little concern to the government beyond ensuring that parliamentary control was reasserted over expenditures. This preoccupation was obvious in the recommendations of the select committee reports of April 1831 and June 1832, and in the general manner in which the Treasury appears to have approached its inquiry.

In his defence, By cited his instructions to ignore the parliamentary grant, and that he had informed the

Ordnance each year what his expenditures would be in the ensuing year. His superiors were well aware before the expenditures were made that the annual grants would be exceeded. With the exception of the £105,000 limit in 1828, his expenditures had never been limited. He had strictly carried out his orders to the best of his ability. By's major defence was that in five years he had constructed a work which would normally have taken 20 years, which was the equal of any canal system in the world, and which was 25 per cent cheaper than any comparable work in North America.

The Ordnance did what it could to defend By against the Treasury onslaught, being well aware of the truth of his claims. Although it could scarcely bring such arguments forward in his defence, comparatively greater cost overruns were being experienced on many Ordnance projects proceeding under far less trying and primitive conditions. The Ottawa canals, for example, which took 15 years to complete, had a cost overrun of 60 per cent on a supplementary estimate submitted in November 1828, and had been running 222 per cent above the original estimate.

Such overruns were typical of major 19th-century construction projects. The Welland Canal took almost ten years to complete at a cost overrun of 55 per cent. The Caledonian Ship Canal, constructed by Thomas Telford, one of the pre-eminent civil engineers of the age, took 19 years to build and incurred an overrun of 87.6 per cent. In contrast, By's cost overrun on the works included in the June 1828 estimate was only 19.7 per cent.

Even if By's cost overrun is regarded in the worst possible light by ignoring the extra works not covered in the June 1828 estimate, his total expenditure of £822,804 was an increase of 42.6 per cent on that estimate and only 18.6 per cent on the March 1830 supplementary estimate accepted by Parliament. This is a far cry from the five-fold increase he was later accused of incurring on the basis of a simple comparison of the preliminary estimate of £169,000 with the final cost.

Nonetheless, the fact remained that a series of estimates for ever-increasing amounts of money had been submitted to Parliament, and in six years a greater sum was spent on the Rideau than on any other Ordnance project in the British Empire to that date. While the cost overruns of many Ordnance projects were relatively far greater than that of the Rideau project, they were spread over an extended period of years and hence were less noticeable. Adjustments could be made in the estimate over time while the day-work system kept expenditures within the annual grants.

In effect, By was betrayed by his own zeal in carrying out his instructions and exploiting the contract system to the utmost. Had construction proceeded at a slower pace, or had he been slower to let his contracts in the spring of 1828 (or perhaps more cautious in letting them in view of the major increase in contemplated expenditures over the woefully inadequate preliminary estimate), the Ordnance might well have been better served. The Kempt Committee then would have been in a position to delay a number of the contracts in keeping with the Ordnance's initial intentions in the spring of 1828. This would have added years to the project, and escalated still further its ultimate cost, but the expenditures would have been kept within the annual grant.

Colonel By was a victim of circumstances beyond his control. Once the project was under way, it was only a matter of time before Parliament would reassert its prerogatives. When the crisis came, the Ordnance was helpless to save By, who deserved a far better fate.

The Ordnance did what it could on By's behalf, including an effort by Sir James Kempt to explain to the government that By had no control over his annual expenditures under the contract system, but it was to little avail. The Treasury inquiry concluded with an expression of regret that By had not curbed his expenditures. Although exonerated, By did not consider that his character and professional reputation had been properly vindicated. In July 1833 he requested the Ordnance to see to it that:

I may be honored with some public distinction as will show that my character as a soldier is without stain, and that I have not lost the confidence or good opinion of my Government.

The Ordnance, to its credit, recommended that By should be presented at a Royal levee as a mark of public recognition for his achievements on the Rideau, but leading members of the Reform government blocked his presentation. Deeply disappointed, and with his health broken by his exertions on the Rideau, By retired to his home in Sussex. He suffered a paralytic stroke a year later and remained bed-ridden until his death at age 56 on February 1, 1836.

Beckett's Landing & Ferry, Long Island Reach or stillwater, Looking towards Long Island, Bytown etc.; [1840s]
Thomas Burrowes, watercolour, 6½" × 10½"
Archives of Ontario

The Rideau River

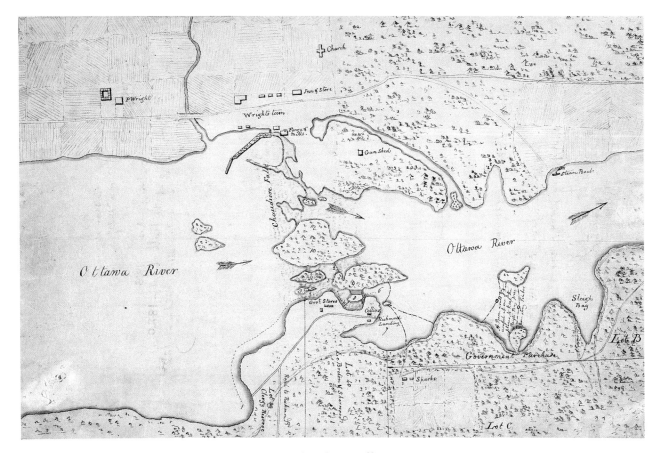

Sketch of both banks of the Ottawa River and the Chaudière Falls

Maj. G. A. Eliot
Public Archives of Canada, C-16156

Col. John By, Royal Engineers; 1830

"C. K."

Royal Engineers Museum

John By was born in England on August 10, 1779. As a youth he entered the Royal Military Academy at Woolwich where he obtained his commission as a second lieutenant in the Royal Artillery just nine days before his 21st birthday. Shortly thereafter he requested, and received, a transfer to the Royal Engineers, the customary procedure for entering that corps.

At Woolwich cadets were given purely theoretical instruction aimed at teaching future artillery and engineering officers the rudiments of their profession. This included such diverse subjects as constructing gun and mortar batteries, erecting fortifications and buildings, surveying and levelling, gunnery, the mechanics of moving and raising great weights, sapping and mining, and making of siege materials, as well as drawing, drafting, trigonometry, geometry, arithmetic, French, and military architecture. After completing the course, cadets joined the Ordnance Survey in Wales for six months of surveying practice before receiving their commissions. They then gained practical experience in the field and after a number of years were expected to be competent in all branches of civil engineering and capable of superintending construction projects, framing estimates and preparing plans for the construction of fortifications, roads, bridges, buildings, telegraph lines, drainage systems, irrigation canals, wharves, storehouses and hospitals.

Over the span of his career By had a wide and varied experience in heavy construction projects, and established a reputation as an officer of great judgment and ability. During an early tour of duty in Lower Canada (1802-11), the then Lieutenant By superintended the construction of the Cascades bateaux canal on the St. Lawrence River, as well as four Martello towers for the defence of Quebec. He also marked himself as an officer of uncommon zeal and initiative when he and a draughtsman-surveyor, Jean-Baptiste Duberger, volunteered to build in their off-duty hours an elaborately detailed scale model of the town of Quebec and its fortifications to aid the Ordnance in preparing future defence plans.

On leaving Quebec By was posted to Portugal under the Duke of Wellington's command where he took part in the first siege of Badajos, May-June 1811. He then returned to England to take charge of the Royal Gunpowder Mills where he supervised the manufacture of gunpowder for the services, as well as the construction of a small-arms factory and several gunpowder presses. In August 1821, as part of a general reduction of army strength, By was retired on half pay at the age of 42.

The Ordnance continued to hold By in high esteem. In December 1824, he was promoted to the rank of lieutenant colonel while still in retirement and in March 1826, he was appointed to superintend the Rideau Canal project — the most difficult and potentially demanding work that the Ordnance had yet to undertake.

A View of the Mill and Tavern of Philemon Wright at the Chaudière Falls, on the Ottawa River, Lower Canada; 1823

Capt. H. Y. DuVernet, Royal Staff Corps, tempera painting, 16¾" × 22½"
Public Archives of Canada, C-608

Following his arrival at Montreal in June 1826, By journeyed up the Ottawa River to the Long Sault Rapids to examine the Grenville Canal project under the direction of Captain Henry DuVernet of the Royal Staff Corps. Once at Grenville, By may well have gone up river to the next obstacle on the Ottawa, the Chaudière Falls, where the thriving village of Wright's Town, or Wrightsville, was situated.

Philemon Wright had arrived at the Chaudière Falls from Woburn, Massachusetts, in March 1800, with a party of 27 settlers to found an agricultural community. Within three years over 300 acres of land was cleared, potatoes, wheat and hemp were growing, and work had started on a grist and hemp mill. By 1806 the settlement was producing a surplus of flour; however, when it was hauled on ox sleighs to Montreal, the price received barely covered the transportation costs. To obtain a cash crop, Wright began to cut timber for rafting to the Quebec export market, a very difficult endeavour as the raft had to be taken apart at each rapids on the Ottawa-St. Lawrence system and the individual sticks hauled overland or shot through the rapids. On his first trip in the spring of 1807, Wright took 25 days just to get his raft by the Long Sault Rapids. Nonetheless, the trip proved profitable and marked the beginning of the timber trade on the Ottawa River.

At about the time By arrived, Wright's Town (renamed Hull in 1875) consisted of a cluster of buildings around a millrace cut from the north shore of the Ottawa River, beside the Chaudière Falls. Among the structures on or near the millrace were a sawmill complex, several grist mills, a blacksmith's forge with four pairs of bellows and a large water-powered hammer, two distilleries, a brewery, a tavern and a three-storey tannery. On the other side of the Britannia Road, which ran from a boat landing below the falls some seven miles to Lake Deschênes on the upper Ottawa, there was a major hotel, the Columbia, a bakehouse, a shoemaker's shop, a tailor shop, a church, eight to ten houses, a school, a major storehouse and a large barn. By 1826 over 800 persons were settled in the town or on nearby farms at a time when major Upper Canadian towns such as Kingston and York (Toronto) had populations of 2849 and 1677 respectively.

Although the difficulties of passing the Ottawa River rapids remained, by 1826, large rafts made up of cribs of squared timber roughly 25 feet wide by 100 feet long with a four-foot draught were carrying several hundred thousand cubic feet of white pine and oak down the river from Wright's Town. The size of the timber trade and the difficulties of getting timber cribs past the rapids did not escape By and they became one more reason for his advocating a large-lock canal system. He argued that if large locks were built, the timber merchants would gladly pay tolls to pass through the locks, rather than risk damaging their timber in the rapids. At a time when the timber trade provided the principal export staple for the British North American colonies, this was a large potential source of revenue.

41

First Camp, Bytown; September 1826

Attributed to Col. John By, R.E., or staff officer, pencil and watercolour, 6¾" × 8⅗
McCord Museum

When By received his orders to begin the Rideau project, he left Montreal by canoe with his staff and arrived at Wright's Town on September 21, 1826. A camp was immediately established on the south side of the Ottawa River at Sleigh Bay, near where the canal would begin. The French-Canadian voyageurs who manned the canoes are shown setting up camp, while the officers in the background toast the new undertaking.

By's establishment was quite small in keeping with the intention to contract out the work. Initially, the Board of Ordnance had assigned one Royal Engineers officer, Captain Daniel Bolton, to By's staff and recommended the hiring of John Mactaggart, a civil engineer experienced in British canal construction, as clerk of works. In Montreal, By had secured the services of another officer, Lieutenant Henry Pooley of the Royal Engineers, as well as three civilian overseers: John Burnett, a superintending engineer from the Lachine Canal project; Thomas Burrowes, a former member of the Royal Sappers and Miners; and John Burrows, a provincial land surveyor. A chief clerk was also taken on. With the exception of Bolton, who was temporarily ill, the new members of By's staff went with him to the Rideau, as did Thomas McKay, a Montreal stonemason and Lachine Canal contractor, who was to assist in selecting potential stone quarry sites.

By the spring of 1827, By's staff totalled 13 men with the addition of an assistant from the light infantry, a clerk of stores, another civilian overseer, a master carpenter and a master smith. In assembling his staff, By appointed only men who were known to be experienced and highly competent.

When he was appointed to the project, By had requested the services of four companies of Royal Sappers and Miners but only two companies, the 15th and 7th, were sent. He also secured three officers from the Kingston garrison to work part-time mapping, sounding and surveying the Cataraqui River above Kingston. During construction, N. H. Baird, a Scots engineer who had worked on the Union Canal at Edinburgh, succeeded Mactaggart as clerk of works when the latter was dismissed for drinking on the job. In 1830 Lieutenant Colonel Boteler of the Royal Engineers was sent by the Ordnance to assist on the Rideau project. Civilian engineers could have been hired, but By believed that they were not as reliable as officers who had been to the Royal Military Academy.

43

Falls of the River Rideau into the Ottawa River; ca. 1826

Thomas Burrowes, watercolour, 7¼" × 10¾"
Archives of Ontario

By's first problem was how to best surmount the Rideau Falls. The twin falls of the Rideau River fell like a curtain — hence the name given them by French-Canadian voyageurs — over a ledge of limestone rock 30 feet above the Ottawa River. Above the falls, the Rideau River was a series of shallows and gentle rapids as far as the Hog's Back Rapids, some five and a half miles inland, and the Three Island Rapids, two and a half miles above the Hog's Back. The water was so shallow that settlers in the Rideau interior often portaged their canoes the whole distance from the Ottawa River to the head of the Hog's Back Rapids.

In 1824 Samuel Clowes recommended that the lower Rideau River and falls be circumvented by building a total of 13 locks, several low overflow dams and five miles of canal cuts to carry traffic from the Ottawa to the deep water above the Three Island Rapids. But much of this excavation would have to be done through solid rock and By was determined to avoid such an expensive, time-consuming plan.

By and Pooley explored the numerous bays along the bank of the Ottawa River to discover a better routing for the canal entrance. Within days they selected Sleigh Bay, upstream from the Rideau Falls at the base of a ravine which stretched back 1090 feet through the high rock cliffs along the Ottawa. At the head of the ravine a large beaver meadow merged into an extensive swamp. By proposed to place eight locks in the ravine to carry the canal up to the level of the beaver meadow, which was to be excavated to form a reservoir for the operation of the entrance locks.

Once the "Entrance Valley" was selected, By set his staff to work surveying and levelling. The water in the swamp appeared to be at roughly the 80-foot level, and he hoped that the canal could be maintained at that level, with a minimum of cutting and embanking, over the seven miles to the Rideau River above the Three Island Rapids. There, By planned to make his junction with the river by constructing three locks to attain the 100-foot level of the deep stillwater at the head of the rapids. By intended to have a sketch map and sections prepared for this first section of the canal by January 1827 so that plans could be prepared and contracts advertised in February. If all went well, the contractors would be ready to start work on the first section at the beginning of the 1827 work season.

On the rest of the canal through to Kingston, By planned to rely for the most part on Clowes's levels and routing. If these were accurate, By was confident that all of the interior works would be contracted out during the summer of 1827.

44

45

Plan & Elevation of the line of Bridges erected at the falls over the Chaudière, Ottawa River; 14 May 1828

Capt. H. I. Savage, R.E.; watercolour, 3¾" × 6"

Dalhousie Muniments, Scottish Record Office, with the permission of The Earl of Dalhousie

Within days of his arrival at the Rideau, By became convinced of the need to connect the Entrance Valley to Wright's Town. He calculated that a series of seven bridges could be erected across the islands in the Ottawa River at the Chaudière Falls for as little as £2000, a far less expensive proposition than employing ferry boats to handle the expected heavy traffic from Hull Township to the Rideau. Another factor was his desire to construct a major bridge on a revolutionary truss design he had developed in 1811.

The bridge project was authorized by the Earl of Dalhousie on September 25, 1826, quarters were rented from the Wrights, and Thomas McKay commenced work immediately on the first stone span with masons from Montreal. When finally completed in September 1828, the crossing, proceeding from the Hull side, consisted of two stone arch bridges of 60-foot span each, an 113-foot-long king-post truss bridge of three spans, a 212-foot-span arched truss bridge over the Great Kettle, an 153-foot-long beam-and-pile bridge reinforced with a king-post truss over the Lost Channel, a short beam bridge over the Devil's Hole, and an 117-foot-span arched truss bridge over the Rafting Channel. A 20-foot-wide macadamized road crossed the bridges.

The Chaudière bridges represent By's first engineering triumph on the Rideau project but it was not achieved without setbacks. The first resulted from a decision to construct the stone span closest to Wright's Town with a low arch of six-foot rise to economize on costs and maximize the width of the arch. To economize further, stone right at the site, only 12 to 13 inches thick, was merely hammer picked and laid in mortar to form the arch. Construction proceeded rapidly, but when the temporary supporting centres were removed on October 31st, the arch collapsed.

McKay was set to work to rebuild it, but first the rise of the arch was increased to 16½ feet and quarries were opened where larger stones were cut and dressed into proper wedges for the voussoirs of the arch. The lateness of the season precluded the use of mortar, so the stone was laid dry by the workmen, who continued their exertions throughout a very severe winter during which their tools and clothing were continually caked in ice from the spray of the falls. The bridge was completed on January 11, 1827, and the second bridge, of similar design and dimensions but with mortared joints, was completed during the summer of 1827.

By planned to construct six stone arched bridges and one wooden truss span (over the Great Kettle), but following an experiment with anchoring a rock-filled timber crib to the riverbed, he became convinced that timber bridge abutments anchored to bedrock would be able to withstand the force of the floodwaters against their base. Accordingly, four wooden truss bridges were erected during the summer of 1827. The contractor, Robert Drummond, was a Montreal stonemason and he also contracted for the Great Kettle bridge.

There, the gap was not only exceedingly wide, 212 feet, but the depth of the water, 72 feet, precluded the erection of scaffolding on the riverbed. A temporary suspension bridge had to be formed for the workmen by shooting a one-inch rope across the gap with a cannon, then

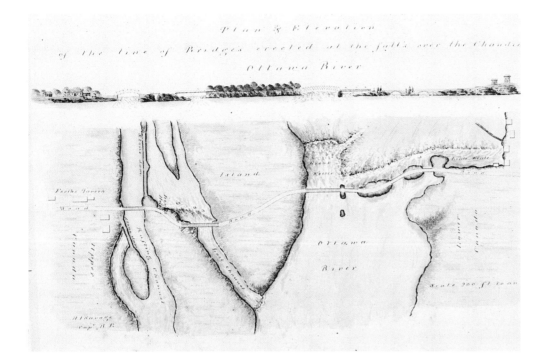

passing larger ropes across on which planks were fixed to form catwalks. To provide support for the arch truss, which was first assembled on shore and then dismantled for re-assembly in position, three chains were drawn across the gap and scaffolding erected on two scows anchored in the river.

This worked well until April 1828, when one and then another of the chains snapped, causing the truss to buckle and tumble into the river. Heavier chains were

Heavier chains were procured from the naval dockyard at Kingston, stronger diagonal bracing was inserted in the the truss, and the joints strengthened. The bridge was completed in September 1828 at almost twice the original £430 estimate.

Although the Bryce Committee would question whether the transport savings effected by the Chaudière bridges justified their cost, By was highly pleased with the undertaking. In October 1828 he forwarded a scale model of the Great Kettle bridge to the Ordnance for presentation to the Duke of Wellington with an explanation of its superiority to truss bridges erected elsewhere. However, it shared the same fate as many early wooden truss bridges. Seven years later the great arch truss began to sag and finally, on May 18, 1836, it collapsed into the river.

Royal Sappers & Miners, Uniform & Working Dress, 1825

George B. Campion, Drawing Master, Royal Military Academy, Woolwich; coloured lithograph, 5¾" × 10," in T. W. J. Connolly, *The History of the Corps of Royal Sappers and Miners* (London: Longman, Brown, Green and Longmans, 1855), Vol. 2, Pl. 13.

Posed against the background of a siege operation, the men in the left foreground are wearing the dress uniforms of the Royal Sappers and Miners; their working dress is shown on the right and in the background. At the far right are two earth-filled cylindrical gabions across which bundles of fascines have been laid to provide cover for the besiegers.

Two companies of sappers and miners, a total of 162 men, arrived at the site of the Rideau project in the summer of 1827. By had hoped for double this number but the expense of maintaining such a large establishment forced him to change his plans. He expected to employ the men in highly skilled construction. The Cornish miners and masons in the ranks, for example, were accustomed to dry keystone work and By had decided that dams on the canal should be built of arched key work without mortar to withstand the severe climate. The force of the water pressing against the outer curve of the horizontal arch would force the stones together. But enough civilian tradesmen were found for the skilled work and the sappers and miners were kept busy guarding stores, keeping order at locksites and completing projects abandoned by private contractors.

It was customary for companies of sappers and miners, raised in England, to be employed on large overseas public works or defence projects in areas where a shortage of skilled tradesmen or very high wage rates made local hiring impractical. The first company, The Soldier Artificers' Company, was formed in 1772 to construct fortifications at Gibraltar. Thereafter a number of companies were recruited from among volunteers in the regular army ranks who could prove that they were competent in one of the trades required. Each company consisted of a set number of men in the various trades as well as non-commissioned officers who were under the command of officers of the Royal Engineers.

The services of sappers and miners were in especially high demand following the Napoleonic Wars as the postwar companies were products of the Royal Engineer Establishment, founded at Chatham in 1812 to instruct the Royal Sappers and Miners, along with the junior officers of the Royal Engineers, in both the theory and practice of constructing fieldworks. For the first time, formal courses of study were established, textbooks prepared, and practical exercises provided in such subjects as constructing gun and mortar batteries, making fascines and gabions, pontooning, arithmetic, general theories of fortification, practical geometry and plan drawing in addition to parade and drills.

Plate XIII

By Town, Upper Canada in 1828; now the City of "Ontario," the seat of Government of the Dominion

[Lt. Edward Frome, R.E.], sepia drawing, 6¼" × 9⅜"
Frome Collection, The Royal Commonwealth Society

The view from Barracks Hill shows Upper Bytown as it appeared in 1828. The Chaudière bridges can be seen in the background as well as Richmond Landing, the small cluster of buildings on the Ottawa just below the Chaudière crossing. In its early years the town was variously referred to as By Town and Bytown, the latter predominating until 1855 when the name was changed to Ottawa. The caption on the drawing, obviously added at a later date, is in error.

Previous to 1826, the site was heavily forested with a thick underbrush, interrupted only by a small settlement at Richmond Landing, where there was a store, tavern, inn and distillery. In 1818 a road was cut through the bush from the river to the Richmond military settlement 20 miles inland. The only other clearing was the farm of Nicholas Sparks near the present corner of Bay and Sparks streets in downtown Ottawa.

In 1824 the Earl of Dalhousie purchased 600 acres along the Ottawa River between the mouth of the Rideau and the bay below Richmond Landing. The land had been granted in 1802 to the son of a Loyalist, who had remained an absentee landowner, and Dalhousie wanted it for the future site of a fortified depot to protect military supplies moving along the proposed Rideau system.

When By arrived in September 1826, Dalhousie turned the property over to him with the admonition that it should be subdivided into lots for lease to half-pay officers, respectable settlers, and tradesmen who would be needed to construct the canal.

Upper Bytown and Lower Bytown, directly east of the Entrance Valley, were surveyed by the engineering staff in October and roads were laid out; the following summer the land was cleared and lots were leased on condition that the lessee construct a house within 12 months of receiving his location ticket. In the spring of 1827, most settlers flocked to Upper Bytown in preference to settling in Lower Bytown, which was in the midst of a heavily wooded, cedar swamp. However, with the construction of drains in 1827 and the influx of labourers and tradesmen seeking work on the canal, Lower Bytown grew more rapidly.

By 1828 there were over 20 frame buildings in Upper Bytown occupied by half-pay officers and relatively well-to-do settlers, but Lower Bytown, with 126 buildings, had surpassed Upper Bytown in population and continued to do so during the canal construction period as a large number of French Canadians settled there in 1828-29 to work on the canal. Irish immigrant workers tended to squat in more primitive temporary accommodations in a settlement called Corktown, which grew up along the canal a mile above the Entrance Valley.

In the Bytown area at the close of 1828 there were ten general mercantile establishments, three bakers, a butcher, three carpenters, three blacksmiths, three watchmakers, eight shoemakers, two tailors, a harness-maker and a tinsmith, all of whom either worked directly on the Rideau project or were dependent on the business it generated for their livelihood. Both sections of Bytown grew rapidly, and in 1835 had a combined population of 1300 inhabitants.

By Town — Upper arcade in 1828
Now the City of "Ontario" — the seat
of government of the Dominion —

51

Entrance to the Rideau Canal from the Cliff, Rideau Barracks; 1832

Lt. Edward Frome, R.E.; sepia drawing, 6½" × 9½"
Frome Collection, The Royal Commonwealth Society

This view from Barracks Hill looks over Sleigh Bay toward the Ottawa River with the wing walls of the first lock of the canal in the right foreground. The high rocky banks made this a natural defensive position, and inspired By to argue that the military depots and naval dockyard at Kingston be moved to Bytown.

The steamboat anchored on the bank, the *Union of the Ottawa*, was the first steamer on the Ottawa River. Built in 1822 by Thomas Mears at Hawkesbury, it ran between Wright's Town and the Long Sault Rapids at Grenville. It was a relatively shallow-draught vessel, 125 feet long with a 28-horsepower engine capable of an average speed of only two and a half miles per hour against the current. The boat wharf in the drawing was built during the fall of 1826 and the depot was erected thereafter. The steamboat at the wharf is probably the *Shannon*, which was launched in 1828.

It is not surprising that By wanted to make the Rideau Canal accessible to steamboats. By the 1820s these vessels were rapidly taking over the passenger and freight business on American waterways and in the Canadas there were several steamers operating on the St. Lawrence, the Ottawa and Lakes Ontario and Erie. It was well known that on the Ohio-Mississippi steamboats attaining speeds of five to seven miles per hour had brought about a virtual economic revolution by drastically reducing the time of transit and freight rates over vast distances, and had been responsible for the rapid development of the American interior.

By also saw the military possibilities of the steamboat and here his intentions went far beyond anything that had been tried before. He proposed a fleet of steamers capable of moving an army of 10,000 men, along with ordnance and supplies, quickly over vast distances. His full plan was not implemented however, and steamboats would not be used on such a scale until the American Civil War (1861-65), when events would show that By's proposal was eminently sound. In the Mississippi Valley, steamboats operating on the major navigable rivers proved superior even to railways in moving and supporting armies in the field. Fleets of up to 80 steamboats were able to move 20,000 men over distances of 450 miles in a week.

First Eight Locks of the Rideau Canal, the North Entrance from the Ottawa River; 1834

Thomas Burrowes, watercolour, 6½" × 10"
Archives of Ontario

The artist is viewing the entrance to the Rideau Canal from the rocky promontory at the eastern edge of Sleigh Bay. The Commissariat building sits to the right of the locks and the Royal Engineers building is directly opposite. On the hill to the left of the Entrance Valley is By's house, with Pooley's house barely visible behind it. Both By and Pooley paid for their houses out of their own pockets.

The steamboat wharf and depot are in the left foreground. Across the Entrance Valley on the right on Barracks Hill are three stone barracks and a hospital. Upper Bytown is in the right background. The buildings on the canal were completed by the fall of 1827, a year after By's arrival.

The flight of eight locks in the centre of the painting carry the canal 80 feet up to the level of the Bytown basin behind the stone arched Sappers Bridge. Originally By planned to construct the locks on the gunboat scale, 20 feet wide by 108 feet long, with an intermediate basin between the fourth and fifth locks.

The excavation contract was let to an Irishman, John Pennyfeather, in April 1827 and the masonry to Thomas McKay in May. Huge boulders, veins of running sand and numerous springs hampered the excavation. Pumps were set to work around the clock and drains constructed to keep the cut clear of water. Nonetheless, excavation proceeded quickly and by December it was two-thirds completed and the masonry floors and part of the side walls were raised on the first three locks.

Masonry work stopped in the spring of 1828 while By waited to learn if locks were going to be enlarged to accommodate steamboats. When the Kempt Committee decided in June that the locks should be 33 feet by 134 feet, the first three locks had to be demolished and the lockpits enlarged. As well, the intermediate basin was eliminated. Masonry work was under way again as of August 1st and the eight locks were completed for testing in the spring of 1831. In September the steamboat *Union* passed through them for the first time.

Of the structures in the painting, only the Commissariat building (now the Bytown Museum) and the locks still exist. The buildings on Barracks Hill were removed prior to the construction of the Parliament Buildings in 1859, and By's and Pooley's houses were both destroyed by fire. The Royal Engineers' building and the Sappers Bridge were demolished in 1912. The lock masonry remained unchanged until the 1920s when the stone facing of locks three through seven was replaced with solid concrete blocks matching the original stone courses.

Lower Bytown, from the Barrack Hill, Near the head of the Eighth Lock and the "Sappers' Bridge": 1845

Thomas Burrowes, watercolour, 6½" × 10"
Archives of Ontario

The extent to which Lower Bytown had grown in just over a decade after the completion of the canal is depicted. Bytown had become the centre of the lumber trade on the Ottawa River and the fastest-growing settlement in the Rideau corridor.

The Sappers Bridge connecting Lower and Upper Bytown was the only bridge crossing the canal below Burritts Rapids until as late as 1867. It had an 18-foot-wide roadway between its parapets and provided a 28-foot clearance over the canal. Beyond the bridge is the elongated Bytown basin which was excavated in the former beaver meadow as a reservoir for the Entrance Valley locks. Above the basin is the deep cut on the Bytown-Dows Lake section of the canal.

In 1844 the Ordnance agreed to sell their town lots in Lower and Upper Bytown to the occupants, and auctioned off the vacant land not required for canal purposes. These transactions were not completed until 1847, prior to which commercial wharfs and warehouses were constructed solely on the Lower Bytown arm of the basin.

The partially hidden building in the foreground of the painting is Thomas McKay's blacksmith's shop. It served as the lockmaster's quarters until a defensible lockmaster's house was constructed in the late 1840s on Ordnance land on the far side of the canal, now Major's Hill Park.

A butcher's shop, bakery, carpenter's shop and blacksmith's shop were erected in this area at the start of the project and the row of buildings enclosed on the Ordnance land to the left of the canal may well be several or all of these structures. In the right foreground is a self-portrait of Thomas Burrowes.

With his customary thoroughness, By organized the operation of the canal well before it opened to traffic and recommended appointees to various positions. When the canal did open in May 1832, members of By's engineering staff were placed in supervisory positions; the lockmasters and lock labourers were drawn from the ranks of the Royal Sappers and Miners and from the civilians who were employed by him. Canal headquarters was located at Bytown and Captain Daniel Bolton, the first appointee to By's staff in 1826, became superintendent. Thomas Burrowes was retained as an overseer of works for the Cataraqui section of the canal, and John Burrows for the Rideau section.

Plan of the Rideau Canal [*Rideau Section*]; *8 July 1830*

Col. John By, R.E.; coloured lithograph
Public Record Office

58

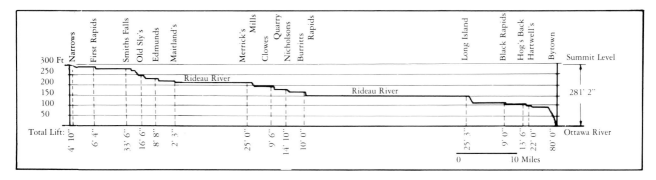

Elevation of the Rideau Canal, Rideau Section
S. Epps
Parks Canada

Hog's Back, Rideau Canal, Upper Canada, 17 August 1830

J. P. Cockburn, watercolour on pencil, 6" × 9⅜"
Public Archives of Canada, C-12515

The scene depicts the thick forest and heavy underbrush in the swampy section between the beaver meadow at the head of the Entrance Valley and the Rideau River near the Hog's Back Rapids. The house in the clearing belongs to either Braddish Billings or Abraham Dow, both of whom settled in the area before the canal was built.

Early in November 1826, John Mactaggart was sent to run a survey from the Entrance Valley inland to the Rideau River above the Hog's Back Rapids. With two assistants, three axemen and two men to carry provisions, Mactaggart intended to explore, sketch and take flying (or quick, rough) levels of the terrain to determine the best routing for the canal. This preliminary survey proved exceptionally difficult and time-consuming: the men had to wade through extensive swamps and water-filled gullies and at times crawled on their hands and knees through the thick underbrush.

They took three days to reach the Rideau River when the same work, Mactaggart noted, 'could have been easily accomplished in a day in England. Under such circumstances a follow-up detailed survey was out of the question. The party withdrew to await the winter freeze-up.

When the ice in the swamps had frozen sufficiently to bear a man's weight, Mactaggart's party resumed its work; however, it was so cold, with temperatures falling as low as -22° F, that the adjustment screws on the theodolite continually froze. The snow was a foot deep and the surveyors, unfamiliar with snowshoes and ice conditions, often broke through and were soaked and frost-bitten. Each evening the party camped at the edge of the swamp in lean-to shelters. The men slept together for mutual warmth "like a parcel of spoons," with their feet to the fire. Often they awoke to find their hair frozen to the ground.

The surveying process was ill-suited to a heavily forested area. In the bush a view of more than 15 feet could not be obtained without the axemen cutting lines of sight. Surveyors had to work literally in the dark where the tops of trees formed an umbrella shutting out the sun. Orientation was also a problem initially as the position, or bearing, of the Three Island Rapids — the ultimate target — was not known with any precision.

On its first penetration into the interior the party had merely moved in the general direction of the Rideau River; now they had to reach a specific point and the only method for fixing its position was by astronomical observations not sufficiently accurate to be useful.

At first Mactaggart was perplexed as to how to obtain a compass bearing for the Three Island Rapids but he quickly hit on a pragmatic solution. He sent men ahead to locate the rapids, where they selected a tall pine tree on high ground and piled firewood around it. The tree was set afire at night, providing a flame which was clearly visible to Mactaggart, seven miles away, giving him a straight-line bearing to his target.

To take flying levels, Mactaggart adopted a method employed by Canadian land surveyors. A candle was placed in a small lantern on the levelling staff, and another placed on the theodolite table. The staff man followed a compass bearing into the bush, and after pacing off a fair distance, lit the candle. When the leveller spotted the candlelight through the sights of the theodolite, he would shout for the staff man to keep the staff in place and would take a reading by the light of the theodolite candle. Before moving on to the next point, the staff man would blow on a horn to guide the surveyor to the position just recorded. This method eliminated much of the laborious work involved in cutting

lines of sight and enabled levels to be read as far as 40 chains
distance (2640 feet).

When the land was later cleared and re-surveyed, the
flying levels corresponded closely to the actual levels.

Hartwell's Locks; ca. 1845

John Burrows, watercolour over pencil, 9" × 12½"
Archives of Ontario

Following completion of the first detailed survey, By planned to carry the canal at the 80-foot level from the Entrance Valley to the Hog's Back where a high dam would block the Rideau and three locks would raise the canal to the level of the water behind the dam. However, it was found that the land beyond the beaver meadow fell into an extensive depression about 470 yards wide and four miles long, Dows Great Swamp, which was inundated with water from the Rideau River in flood time. On the far side of the swamp the land rose into the Nepean Hills that extended to the Hog's Back about five miles from the Entrance Valley.

Determining the best route for a canal and an efficient layout for the canal structures was one of the most demanding tasks in 19th-century civil engineering. It required skill and judgment, exhaustive survey work and a minute exploration of the terrain. The object was to find not only a practicable route, but one which would best preserve the level desired with an absolute minimum of excavating and embanking over the shortest possible distance. Even with the best of planning, changes were commonly made during construction, as was the case of the first section of the Rideau Canal, to take full advantage of the terrain.

Between the Entrance Valley and Dows Swamp two canal cuts were made, joined by a natural gulley, and two parallel mounds were erected across Dows Swamp using clay from the canal excavations. The mounds were about 880 yards apart and between them raised the water level to form Dows Lake. Two of the three locks intended for Hog's Back were moved to Hartwell's where higher ground began beyond the lake. With the canal raised 22 feet at Hartwell's, it was possible to follow a straight cut directly to the Hog's Back with a minimum of excavation.

The locks at Hartwell's are shown in this painting. Each had a lift of 11 feet and was built by Thomas McKay. To the left of the upper lock is a masonry waste weir carrying surplus water into the Rideau River a short distance away. A defensible lockmaster's house, erected in the early 1840s, stands to the right of the upper lock. A number of schooners plied the canal during its first decade of operation but were thereafter totally superseded by steamboats.

Today at Hartwell's a second storey has been added to the lockmaster's house and the whole structure clapboarded, hiding its military characteristics. The waste weir was replaced with an underground concrete culvert and during the 1920s the stone facing of the upper lock was replaced by concrete blocks.

Dam at the Hog's Back, shewing the Breach in the Stone-Work in 1830 [sic] — Sketched in July 1845 from the Bed of the River

Thomas Burrowes, watercolour, 6½" × 10"
Archives of Ontario

The painting purports to show the Hog's Back dam a year after it was breached by floodwaters in April 1829. Many of the heavy stones carried away by the flood are visible in the foreground.

The Hog's Back Rapids were named for a ridge of limestone that imperiled the rafts of logs that shot down the Rideau River on the high water each spring. The river was 170 feet wide at the Hog's Back, with a discharge of about 170,000 cubic feet per minute, and in flood the boiling water rose 16 feet up its banks. By decided to take advantage of the lofty riverbanks at the spot by throwing a 45-foot-high dam across the channel to flood the Three Island Rapids further upstream and provide a navigable depth of water all the way to Black Rapids, four miles away. The plan was a bold one, given the turbulent water at the site, and a series of disasters eventually brought By to despair of ever completing it.

The contractor, Walter Fenelon of New York, began work on the dam in July 1827. Dumping earth and loose stone fill into the river from the east bank, Fenelon began to build up a masonry arch against the downstream side of the fill. Stones were laid dry and fitted tightly — or keyed — together on end, with a 20-foot-wide core wall of clay puddle between the masonry and the fill. By the autumn Fenelon had raised the earth dam and masonry keywork to a height of 37 feet and extended it across the channel to within 60 feet of the west bank. This gap was filled with earth and stone but in February 1828, a sudden flood washed away the fill, opening the gap and causing Fenelon to abandon the project.

By rushed the 15th company of Royal Sappers and Miners to the Hog's Back and a rock-filled timber crib was rapidly built across the gap from the west bank to overlap the end of Fenelon's unfinished dam. This was no sooner in place than a second disaster struck. Floodwaters on March 29th turned the end of the timber crib and washed out tons of clay from the west bank of the river. Refusing to give up, By resumed work once the spring floods subsided and in a year's time the project was again well advanced when for a third time floodwaters tore through the dam. This is the setback shown in the painting.

At this point By abandoned plans for a keywork dam and instead extended the timber-crib portion across the entire channel. The height of the dam was increased to 49 feet to prevent water ever flowing over it and a permanent waste weir was built to control the floodwaters. One hundred and sixty men went to work on the project in July 1829 and two years later, in the summer of 1831, the 250-foot-long Hog's Back dam was finished.

Hog's Back; ca. 1845

John Burrows, watercolour over pencil, 9" × 12½"
Archives of Ontario

The canal cut from Dows Lake can be seen joining the Rideau River beside the Hog's Back Rapids. Two locks were constructed: a lift lock raising the canal 13 feet 6 inches and a guard lock at the upper end. On waterways where the upper lock in a canal cut was exposed to the full brunt of a river in flood, it was customary to construct a set of guard gates, or a guard lock (with no lift), in front of the upper lock as a safety precaution. Originally By provided for a guard lock at all the locksites between Hog's Back and Long Island. Later he eliminated all but the one at Hog's Back where he feared the effects that such a high head of water might have on the lower structures if the gates of the lift lock should be damaged.

Walter Fenelon, the original contractor for the Hog's Back dam, also contracted for the locks as well as the excavation work between the Entrance Valley and the Hog's Back. Fenelon won the contracts because he was by far the lowest bidder but he had no experience in masonry work and eventually could not finish the work. Fenelon's experience was common among contractors on the canal. Contracts were supposed to be awarded only to men of known competence in the type of work to be undertaken, but under the pressures of time and economy By frequently violated his own rules. The results were predictable: contractors defaulted at a number of locksites. At Hog's Back the job had to be contracted out again at slightly higher rates.

Today, the canal and locks at the Hog's Back remain as they were constructed. The original waste weir has long since been replaced by a succession of timber-crib and then concrete structures. In 1886 a timber swing bridge was constructed across the guard lock and a fixed bridge over the waste weir to provide a road crossing. The high dam has become obscured over the years by dredging debris dumped to strengthen it. A defensible lockmaster's house was constructed at the Hog's Back during the 1840s. It stood just inside the picket fence at the right of the picture, and was demolished early in the present century.

Lock, Dam &c at Black Rapids, Men pumping Water out of the Lock, to hang the Gates &c &c; September 1830

Thomas Burrowes, watercolour, 6½" × 9¾"
Archives of Ontario

At Black Rapids, some four miles upstream from the Hog's Back, the river was about 275 feet wide but as little as two feet deep in the summer, and it was broken by a half mile of boulder-strewn rapids. The contract for the locksite was let in June 1827 to two Montreal contractors, Thomas Phillips and Andrew White, who opened a stone quarry on the east bank of the river, about 700 yards beyond the dam, and cleared the locksite on the west side of the river.

By planned to construct only a 13-foot-high overflow dam, to back up the water at a navigable depth to the Long Island locksite five miles upstream, and a single lock. No waste weir was planned for Black Rapids, or any of the other Rideau Canal locksites, as the overflow dam was intended to maintain the requisite level of water in the canal year round.

In the spring of 1829, floodwaters poured over the newly completed Black Rapids dam, severely damaging the soft bedrock at its base and raising the spectre of its being undermined over time. Since the dam was one of the lowest planned for the entire system, By was forced to reconsider the concept of permitting floodwaters to flow over the dams. He decided to raise the height of the high dams to prevent water flowing over them, and to construct waste weirs at those sites to carry off the surplus water. Where the low dams were concerned, as at Black Rapids, the overflow principle was maintained, but waste weirs were also constructed to carry off the floodwaters.

At the close of 1830, all of the Black Rapids structures were completed. These consisted of a stone arch overflow dam, a single masonry lock of nine-foot lift, and a masonry waste weir. In the painting, the men are moving the lower pair of lock gates into place by means of a block and tackle. To the right can be seen the road from the Entrance Valley and a stone lockmaster's house which was used as an office during the construction period. Two log bunkhouses were also built, one of which is shown.

With the exception of the lock chamber, none of the structures in the drawing have survived. The log buildings disappeared by mid-century and the lockmaster's house was removed in 1914. A timber-crib dam replaced the stone dam in 1862 and the present concrete dam was constructed in three stages over the years 1949-54. The original waste weir was repaired extensively in 1917 and replaced in concrete in 1925. The lock chamber walls were also largely rebuilt with a concrete block facing in 1928, and hydraulic cylinders were installed in 1969 to work the lock gates.

Richmond, on the River Jacques, or Goodwood, a tributary of the Rideau River, Septr 1830

Thomas Burrowes, watercolour, 6¼" × 10½"
Archives of Ontario

At the close of the War of 1812, a pressing concern for the British government was where to place discharged regular officers and soldiers, as well as militiamen, so that they might become self-supporting in the postwar period. A Military Settling Department was established to select strategically important sites for settlement, and to provide transport and support for the veterans and their families while they settled on the land. The establishment of settlements to the rear of the proposed Rideau Canal was given a top priority.

To encourage disbanded regiments to settle in the Rideau interior, free land grants were offered according to rank with officers receiving 600 to 800 acres and privates 100 acres. To promote further settlement and alleviate the high postwar unemployment in Britain, the British government in 1815 offered assistance to any Britons wishing to emigrate. Emigrants were given free passage and provisions on the journey, and once in Upper Canada, received a land grant and a loan of £10, to be repaid before the settler received title to his land. Each immigrant and military family was given all of the tools required to clear the land, build a house and sow a crop.

In May 1815 the first group of 700 persons left Scotland for the Perth military settlement on the Pike (Tay) River, and each year the number increased through to 1821 when over 1800 emigrants arrived in the military settlements under the assisted emigration scheme. Initially the British government planned to support each family during only their first year on the land, but the killing of the first potato crop by frost in 1817 and rust damage to the wheat crop made the Perth settlers dependent on continued government rations during the "hungry times."

The drawing shows the military settlement at Richmond from the vantage point of the Richmond Road bridge. Early in the summer of 1818, the 99th Regiment of Foot was disbanded at Quebec. The officers and men and their families went by bateaux to Bellow's Landing (then renamed Richmond Landing) at the foot of the Chaudière Falls. From there the men cut a road 20 miles through the bush to the Jock River, a branch of the Rideau known originally as the Jacques or the Goodwood. A village was surveyed and named in honour of the Duke of Richmond. A Commissariat store was erected to dispense rations, tools and blankets to the settlers and a saw and grist mill was quickly built. The Richmond Road was carried across the Jock and through the bush a further 30 miles to the Perth military settlement. Richmond did not grow as rapidly as Perth, but five years after Burrowes made this sketch, Richmond had a population of 200.

By 1822 the settlements were well established and self-supporting, and both the Military Settling Department and the assisted emigration scheme were discontinued. In 1822 the Perth and Lanark settlements alone had a combined population of 10,700, including 3570 males of whom 1300 were veterans. These settlements, in conjunction with the Richmond settlement, were counted on to provide a labour force, as well as tools, food and fodder for the Rideau Canal construction sites.

Saw-Mill Frame & Log Dam at the Foot of Long Island: Sketched 15 June 1827, when Surveying for Location of the Works

Thomas Burrowes, watercolour, 6¾" × 9½"

Archives of Ontario

The Long Island sawmill, owned by a Mr. Hulbert, was out of operation in June 1827 when the Royal Engineers began their survey of the area. Although the lands along the Rideau were sparsely settled, a number of saw and grist mills were in operation at several waterfalls.

Lumbering began on the river in 1810 when Braddish Billings, who had worked for Philemon Wright cutting timber and oak staves on the upper Ottawa River, built a shanty on the lower Rideau below the Hog's Back. Billings cleared some land but farming was secondary to lumbering. Logs were hand squared with axes and adzes and floated out on the spring floods for sale to Philemon Wright and Sons. Billings was the only settler in Gloucester, on the eastern bank of the river, until circa 1819 when several families moved into the township to settle on the land.

The existence of mills on the Rideau posed a problem as the surveyors had to lay out the canal without leaving the government liable for heavy damages or having to buy out the water privileges of mill owners. This was just one of the things which made John Burrows's job difficult as he toured the route making notes and rough sketch maps. He had to report where the river would have to be cleared, where coffer dams were required and the type of soil and rock which had to be excavated.

At each rapid Burrows made sketches locating the various obstacles to navigation, and the proposed line of canal through or around them. He commented on the potential layout and location of the structures required to overcome the rapids, and the general cost and difficulty of constructing them. Stone quarries were located and occasionally Burrows noted how a saving might be realized by re-positioning locks to take advantage of the terrain or raising a dam to reduce the amount of rock excavation.

Another of Burrows's responsibilities was to determine the amount of damage which might be done to potentially good farm land or existing buildings and property by raising the water levels. He noted where the riverbanks were particularly low and estimated the number of acres of land which would be inundated in each instance.

Long Island Rapids; 5 May 1828

Col. John By, R.E.; coloured drawing, 4" × 6"

Dalhousie Muniments, Scottish Record Office, with the permission of The Earl of Dalhousie

At Long Island, according to the site plan of May 1828, By planned to build a stone arched dam across the shallows near the foot of the rapids and three combined locks adjacent to the dam in a short canal cut. A long, 10-foot-high earthen embankment was to cross a ravine to prevent the raised water from escaping. As was so often the case, the plan had to be amended. The dam originally intended to be arched only across the deep portion of the riverbed was arched from bank to bank. It was also increased to 31 feet high and the total lift of the locks was increased to 25 feet 3 inches. A waste weir was placed in a channel cut from above the dam to Mud Creek, which entered the Rideau a short distance downstream of the dam. The dam and embankment formed a stillwater 25 miles long to Burritts Rapids.

The Long Island site is typical of the construction technique By adopted after he completed his initial survey. Clowes had recommended that rapids be surmounted with locks in canals cut around the rapids or with separate locks placed adjacent to a series of low overflow dams stepping up through the rapids. By abandoned this approach. Instead he constructed a slackwater system in which high dams raised the water level to flood the rapids and back up the water to a navigable depth. Each stillwater so created would stretch upriver to the base of the dam at the next set of rapids.

By's approach was unprecedented. The slackwater system of canal construction was virtually unknown in England where 18th-century canals were constructed in cuts made independent of rivers, which were used only as feeders for the canals. In the United States slackwater systems had been built, but none were near the scale that By proposed, with dams up to 60 feet high. Indeed, slackwater systems on the scale of the Rideau would have been impossible in either England or the United States because of land values. On the Rideau route, however, no such problem existed since either the natural riverbanks were high enough to retain the raised water with a minimum of embanking or the areas to be flooded were mostly low-lying rock or marshy swamp.

The construction of a slackwater system complicated the surveying task but it reduced excavation work immensely. The 25 miles of canal cuts required by Clowes's plan were reduced to eight and half miles in total, and the depth of the excavations was also reduced considerably. John Mactaggart, the Clerk of Works, stated that if Clowes's plan had been followed, it would have bankrupted the British Treasury. More probably it would have resulted in the eventual abandonment of the project in an unfinished state.

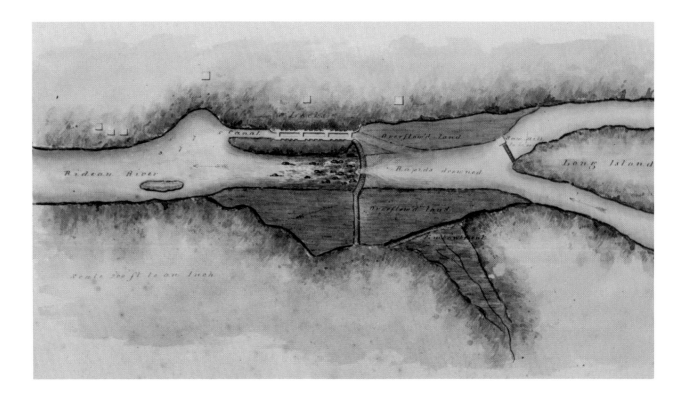

Long Island; ca. 1845

John Burrows, watercolour over pencil, 8⅝" × 10⅞"
Archives of Ontario

Prior to the construction of the canal works, the Rideau River was not navigable on either side of Long Island. Along the length of the island the river channels dropped 25 feet and were strewn with rapids and shallows which in summer were as little as six inches deep. Long Island was situated in the midst of a wilderness which stretched virtually uninterrupted from the Ottawa River to Burritts Rapids. The nearest settlement was Richmond, 20 miles up the Jock River, which entered the Rideau about one mile below Long Island. There was a small settlement at Burritts Rapids, 25 miles above Long Island, and a clearing on the river in between where several lumbermen and their families had settled in 1820-23 to cut timber.

Once By agreed to construct a supply road from the Entrance Valley to Long Island, the works were contracted out at moderate prices to Thomas Phillips and Andrew White, who began clearing the locksite in July 1827. The only major difficulty on the works was procuring stone for the masonry structures. Initially stone was quarried directly on the site, but the hard grey rock found there was difficult to cut and stone had to be sledged in from the Black Rapids and Hog's Back quarries during the winter months.

The watercolour provides a view of Long Island lockstation as it appeared in the 1840s. The three combined locks lie in a short canal cut adjacent to the high arch dam. The waste weir originally constructed at the head of the channel to the right of the dam was swept away by floodwaters in 1836 and replaced by the timber-crib waste weir on which the road bridge is built. The house on the knoll beside the locks is the lockmaster's house and behind it can be seen the beginnings of the village of Long Island.

This village sprang up in the immediate post-construction period but it did not continue to grow. After two decades, changes made in the water-control system at Long Island brought about its demise. In 1858 a new waste weir was constructed from the lower tip of Long Island to the embankment adjacent to the dam, and an additional waste weir was built across the west channel of the river where a grist mill was immediately erected to use the waterpower it provided. The mill drew settlers to the new dam site and by 1860, with the founding of the village of Manotick, the Long Island village was all but deserted.

Today the dam at Long Island stands as originally constructed, but the lockmaster's house, ancillary canal structures, and the early dwellings have long since disappeared. The waste weirs constructed in 1858 have been rebuilt in concrete and the lock chambers were re-faced in the 1920s with concrete blocks formed to resemble the original cut-stone facing.

Rideau Canal, Long Island on the Rideau River; August 1830

J. P. Cockburn, watercolour on pen and ink, 14¼" × 10⅝"
Royal Ontario Museum

The central figure is dressed in the distinctive fashion of the Irish immigrants who worked on the canal. Instead of ordinary trousers, the Irish wore the older style breeches with knee stockings and a simple shirt. The black silk stovepipe hat is also typically Irish. An axe was a constant companion of any settler travelling through the bush in Upper Canada. This man and his wife were presumably squatters on land along the canal route and living in the rude hovel.

Thousands of Catholic Irish began to arrive in British North America after 1825 because of economic conditions in their own country. Many gravitated to canal projects in the United States looking for work and a large number came to the Rideau project, which employed over 4000 men at any one time. The Irish became a large component of that labour force, along with men and boys from the interior settlements and a significant number of French Canadians.

The life of a labourer on the Rideau project was extremely arduous. Not only did he work 14- to 16-hour days, six days a week, as was customary in the early 19th century, but he did so under the most primitive and taxing of conditions. There were few labour-saving devices. Once the line of canal was selected, axemen cut the trees and oxen dragged the logs and boulders off the site. Then excavation began with pick, shovel and wheelbarrow.

Stumps were removed as the excavation reached them by workers digging underneath to drop them into the cut so they could be hauled away, but this was exceptionally dangerous as the stumps frequently fell on the men below. Rock excavation required much laborious drilling to set the charges and blasting resulted in deaths and serious injuries.

Long hours of incessant pumping also were required to keep the excavations clear of water.

Labourers were well fed, in keeping with the heavy work demanded of them, but their living conditions were such as bred disease. Skilled labourers were boarded with local settlers, but others were cooped up in log bunkhouses. Several two-storey shanties, 30 by 40 feet, often housed up to 200 workers at the major locksites. On many sections of the canal, men lived in swamps where they were not only plagued with mosquitoes, black flies and dysentery, but also ran a high risk of contracting malaria.

Through all the afflictions endured by labourers on the Rideau project, it was the Irish immigrants who suffered the most. They arrived at the Rideau in poor health, following a long voyage in crowded, disease-ridden ships, with nothing but rags and the clothing on their backs to protect them from the elements. In such a condition, they were particularly susceptible to disease and their mortality rate was high. Moreover, whether through ignorance or improvidence, the Irish labourers generally made no effort to prepare for the severe North American winter, and often refused to purchase the blankets, bedding and clothing that the Commissariat offered.

As a consequence, they suffered during the work season and the winter when they lived in rude huts or caves in the riverbank on the outskirts of Bytown and Kingston. With no income and clothing poorly suited to the Canadian climate, they suffered terribly from the cold, hunger and sickness that decimated their numbers and left the survivors even more susceptible to illness. In contrast, local settlers and French Canadians, who were better dressed to withstand the winter cold, simply returned to

their homes to await the next season or migrated to the timber shanties to get jobs in the timber trade.

No doubt in large part because of the brutal conditions under which they lived and worked, the Irish were noted for their heavy drinking and brawling. Innumerable brawls and several pitched battles took place between the Irish labourers and the local farmers, and between different groups of Irish labourers. Their unruly behaviour forced By to deploy the Royal Sappers and Miners to maintain order. At Bytown a sergeant and 12 men guarded the Commissariat stores from the Irish. Chronically short of supplies, they would take whatever they needed if not restrained by the presence of armed guards.

Following the completion of the canal, few Irish settled in the area. They generally preferred wage labour to farming and either departed for the cities and other canal projects looking for work, or gravitated to Bytown where they eventually gained employment rafting timber down the Ottawa.

Burritt's Rapids; ca. 1840s

John Burrows, watercolour, 8¾" × 12½"
Archives of Ontario

At Burritts Rapids, 25 miles above the Long Island dam, the nature of the Rideau changed abruptly. The heavily forested land of the lower river, with its high rocky banks at the Hog's Back and low marshy banks on the long stillwater above Long Island, gave way to a long stretch of low-lying land highly suitable for cultivation. Above Burritts Rapids the river ran through a series of rapids, dropping 60 feet overall. This was the area of the "Lower Rideau Settlement," where individual Loyalist families settled as early as the 1790s at mill sites subsequently known as Burritts Rapids, Nicholsons Rapids, and Merrick's Mills. One of the early settlers was Colonel Stephen Burritt who had served with Roger's Rangers during the American Revolution and came to the rapids in 1793.

The low banks at Burritts Rapids precluded the construction of a dam across the river to flood the rapids and shallows; By was forced to revert to Clowes's system of a canal cut bypassing the rapids in conjunction with a low overflow dam across the river to deepen the water at the upper entrance to the cut. However, By planned to take advantage of an existing snye, or dry flood channel, to minimize the excavation and embanking work. At the lower end of the snye, where the water backed up by the Long Island dam was a navigable depth, By constructed a single lock to raise the water level ten feet. That level was maintained throughout the one-and-a-half-mile length of the snye.

The excavation and masonry work at Burritts Rapids, let to Philemon Wright and Sons on February 1, 1828, proceeded rapidly. The major work was in blasting rock to deepen the snye and in constructing two embankments. To economize on expenditures, a wooden lock floor was substituted for the planned masonry floor and the stone

arched overflow dam intended for the site was replaced by a straight dam, 240 feet long, constructed of timber braces and stop logs. No waste weir was constructed at Burritts Rapids because the bedrock in the river seemed capable of withstanding the force of floodwater pouring over the eight-foot-high dam.

The dam is not visible in the watercolour, but the river can be seen flowing downstream from the right, the high embankment in the centre raising the waters in the canal channel above the lock. The building on the river at the far right is a grist mill erected at Burritts Rapids prior to the construction of the canal. The high-level bridge had a 28-foot clearance over the canal. The two buildings on the canal bank below the bridge probably housed canal workers.

A defensible lockmaster's house, next to the lock, was constructed following the 1837 rebellions when there was a fear that marauders from bases in the United States might attempt to damage or destroy works along the Rideau Canal. The buildings to the left, separated from the Ordnance land at the lockstation by the picket fence, are the beginnings of a small settlement; however, the future site of the village of Burritts Rapids was on the other side of the river a short distance beyond the grist mill.

Nicholson's Rapids; ca. 1840s

John Burrows, watercolour over pencil, 9" × 12¼"
Archives of Ontario

Nicholsons Rapids is located about three miles above Burritts Rapids. It was settled first in 1785 by Robert Nicholson, a Loyalist from Albany, New York, who served with Jessop's Rangers in the American Revolution.

Construction at Nicholsons Rapids proved troublesome. First of all, Clowes's levels were grossly in error, forcing By to modify his original plans for the site. Once again instead of flooding the rapids with a high dam, By had to place a low dam, nine feet high, at the head of the rapids and excavate a canal cut in the steep bank of the river. Two locks, of a combined lift of 14 feet, 10 inches, were constructed and pumps were going almost continuously to keep the canal excavation free of water which seeped through the loose rock. Since the river bedrock was too soft to withstand the full crest of floodwaters pouring over the dam, a waste weir was built near the head of the canal cut.

In the 1840s, when this watercolour was done, a storehouse stood beside the lower lock and, on the knoll, a defensible lockmaster's house erected in 1838. The several buildings just above the upper lock housed canal workers during the construction period, and one of these served as a lock labourer's house. The bridge in the foreground was used to bring stone from Clowes Quarry to the lockpits. Two houses (to the far left) were erected by Robert Nicholson.

Much of the farmland around Nicholsons Rapids was cleared and settled within a decade of the canal's construction. With the establishment of a flour mill by Rufus Andrews in 1861, the small village of Andrewsville grew up a short distance from the bridge in the right foreground. In 1864 Andrews erected a swing bridge across the canal cut to complete the road crossing. That swing bridge was replaced with a wooden king-post truss swing bridge, a facsimile of which is still in operation.

The flour mill was demolished in 1917 and the fixed bridge replaced about that time with a steel bridge. The storehouse at the lower lock has also long since been removed, but the defensible lockmaster's house still survives. The dam remains as originally built, but a concrete facing was applied to its upstream face in 1913 and a concrete apron was added there in 1975-76. The stonework of the waste weir was totally renewed in 1907.

Clowes' Quarry; 1832

John Burrows, pencil sketch, 6" × 14¾"
Public Archives of Canada, C-11164

At the rapids at what became known as Clowes Quarry, a single lock of nine-foot six-inch lift was constructed on the west bank of the river, with a waste weir adjacent to the lock and an overflow dam abutting the waste weir. The 300-foot stone arched dam, 15 feet high, created a two-mile-long stillwater which carried the canal at a navigable depth to Merrickville. The riverbed was deepened by excavating rock for a distance of 130 yards downstream from the lockpit.

The buildings on the far side of the river were built to house canal workers employed at the locksite. The dwellings on the near bank include the original home of James Clowes, one of the pre-canal settlers in the area, as well as a building that housed the workers who were employed in his quarry. By contracted with Clowes for preliminary work at the rapids and during the summer of 1827 Clowes cleared the locksites and opened an excellent limestone quarry which provided stone for the canal works at Burritts Rapids, Nicholsons, Clowes Quarry and Merrick's Mills. Clowes also received a contract for the excavation and masonry work at the site, but he proceeded to construct the dam in such an unworkmanlike manner that By had no choice but to break the contract in January 1828. The following month the works were re-contracted to Alexander Hays.

At Clowes Quarry changes were made in conventional construction techniques which resulted in substantial amounts of money being saved. Clay puddle proved very expensive to procure on this section of the canal, and after a flood in the spring of 1828 drove much of the puddlework through the unfinished keywork of the dam, broken stone from the quarry was substituted for the conventional clay-puddle core. When compacted, it proved equally impermeable and a good deal cheaper. The structure of the lock was also modified to take advantage of the rock foundation at the base of the lockpit and on the riverbed above.

As was customary at other locksites where the bedrock was sound, the floor of the Clowes lock consisted simply of bare rock with an oak sill anchored to the bedrock at the lower gates. However, at Clowes the lockpit floor was levelled through to the wing walls at the upper end of the lock, and an oak sill was anchored at the upper gates on the same level as the lower sill. To step up from the lock floor to the riverbed above the lock, stop logs were permanently fixed in the stop-log grooves of the upper wing walls up to the height of the bedrock in the river above. The gap between the stop-log wall and the end of the lockpit excavation was then filled with small stones laid in cement. This unorthodox procedure saved the expense of some 9300 cubic feet of masonry that would otherwise have been required to construct a breastwork in the upper end of the lock.

Initially, By planned to construct the Clowes Quarry lock on the east bank of the river to match the locks at Nicholsons only half a mile downstream, but a hard compact rock was encountered which necessitated the lock being moved to the west bank where the excavation proceeded in clay and earth. The waste weir was positioned between the lock and dam, as at Black Rapids, but with one improvement: it was angled so that the water would shoot out into the centre of the river away from the lock wall.

Cohoes' Quarry
1832

85

Block house at Merrickville on the Rideau Canal between Bytown and Kingston, Upper Canada, finished March 1839

Capt. H. F. Ainslie, 25th Regiment of Foot
Public Archives of Canada, C-512

From the inception of the Rideau project, By was conscious of the need to defend the canal, but no steps were taken until June 1828 when the Kempt Committee instructed him to determine what lands would be required for military purposes, purchase the lands if possible, and construct the lockmasters' houses as defensible guardhouses, pending a decision on future major fortifications. By preferred blockhouses to guardhouses and in March 1830 forwarded to the Ordnance a blockhouse proposal which, if approved with the military land purchases required, would add a further £69,230 to the Rideau estimate.

In view of the heavy expenditures on the project, the Ordnance postponed any major defensive works on the Rideau, but neglected to inform By of that decision until the spring of 1832. In the interim, he contracted for the construction of several blockhouses on the grounds that they were absolutely necessary. These structures were located at Merrickville, the Narrows on the Rideau Lakes, the Isthmus at the summit of the canal and Kingston Mills. A fifth contract was made for a blockhouse at Burritts Rapids but it was not completed because of financial restraints.

By was acutely concerned with defending the Merrick's Mills canal works. Not only had a good road been developed between Merrick's Mills and the Brockville Road, but the provincial government began to upgrade the Prescott Road in the spring of 1832. In effect, the wilderness buffer that the Ordnance wanted maintained between the Rideau and St. Lawrence was to be breached by an excellent road that offered an enemy force easy access to the canal.

The Merrickville blockhouse, shown in this picture, was the first constructed on the canal. Although smaller than By originally proposed, it was far larger than later ones and much more closely approximated his preferred design. It stood beside the upper lock with a wooden ramp providing access to a single door facing the lock. A single gun port was built into each wall of the masonry lower storey for mounting a cannon, and all four sides of the timber upper storey had openings for small-arms fire. Loopholes, called machicolations, were also cut in the underside of the overhang to enable the defenders to fire at any attackers reaching the walls. Pending an outbreak of hostilities, the loopholes were stopped with plank plugs and windows were framed in the gun ports.

Beside the blockhouse is the rolling bridge erected over the upper lock to carry the Brockville Road extension and the Prescott Road, both of which crossed the Rideau at Merrickville. The king-post truss bridge, at the far right, carried the road over the snye to the milldam. The storage sheds behind the blockhouse postdate canal construction and are separated by a picket fence from the commercial building just beyond the Ordnance land. It is not known what the raised cylindrical object above the lock is supposed to be; early maps show nothing in that area. The painting is not accurate in detail, but does show the position and main characteristics of the blockhouse.

The upper storey of the Merrickville blockhouse housed the lockmaster and his family. In the event of war, the blockhouse was intended to be a mustering point for

the local militia, a supply depot where provisions, ammunition and arms could be stored, and a strong defensive position for repelling anyone attempting to destroy the canal structures. If needed, it could accommodate a garrison of 50 men; however, guns were never mounted in it and it served a military function only once. In the aftermath of the 1837 rebellion, when British troops were rushed to Upper Canada via the Rideau Canal, the blockhouse was taken over temporarily by the 34th Regiment which was enroute to Fort Malden at Amherstburg.

During the Oregon crisis of 1846 when war with the United States threatened, it was designated as the headquarters for the Rideau line of defence and a key fall-back position should the St. Lawrence front be abandoned, but it was not garrisoned by regular troops and continued to serve as a lockmaster's residence until the late 19th century. Thereafter, the building was not kept up and the impending collapse of the roof necessitated the removal of the second storey in 1908-09. In 1960-65 it was restored to its former appearance and turned into a museum.

Merrick's Mills; ca. 1840s

John Burrows, watercolour over pencil, 9" × 12½"
Archives of Ontario

At Merrick's Mills, 45 miles from Bytown, settlement began in 1792 when William Merrick, a Loyalist millwright from Massachusetts, cut a path through the bush from Prescott and began a sawmill at the "Great Falls" where the Rideau fell 14 feet. After an initial failure, Merrick succeeded in building a sawmill and grist mill with a 12-foot-high dam backing up the main river channel. During the 1790s a number of families moved inland to settle in the surrounding area, which by 1820 was the most heavily populated section on the whole Rideau waterway.

In Wolford and Montague townships, which included most of the Lower and Upper Rideau Settlements on either side of the river, over 530 persons were settled on the land, and at Merrick's Mills, in addition to the saw and grist mills, there was a general store, a blacksmith's shop, a tavern, a storehouse, and several private dwellings. By 1829 Merrick's Mills was flourishing and sufficiently populated to be designated a village under the name Merrickville.

At Merrickville the canal cut was excavated on the east bank of the river and an overflow dam was constructed across the river at the head of the cut above the millpond so the mill complex was left relatively undisturbed. To minimize the excavation required, the canal cut was carried along the slope of the riverbank where excavating and embanking could be balanced, and the locks were positioned along the slope to minimize the depth of the cut. To save money, the overflow dam was constucted of timber braces and stop logs, as at Burritts Rapids and First Rapids (Poonamalie), rather than of arched masonry. The dam, anchored to the sloping bedrock of the river, was six to ten feet high and 180 feet long. The dam and locks were constructed by A. C. Stevens, the contractor at Nicholsons Rapids.

The three detached locks are shown in the watercolour. The locks, with a combined lift of 25 feet, and the dam across the river (not shown) formed a stillwater of navigable depth stretching eight and a quarter miles upstream to Maitland's Rapids (Kilmarnock). At the upper lock, a blockhouse protected the canal works and a rolling bridge restored a road communication that passed over the fixed bridge across the waste-water channel and along the top of the milldam in the main river channel. (Both the fixed bridge and milldam predated the canal.)

By the 1840s the complex adjacent to the milldam included a sawmill, two grist mills, a carding mill, a distillery and an axe factory. On the east bank of the canal cut opposite the lower lock is the log building erected to provide an office for the Royal Engineers and accommodation for a detachment of Royal Sappers and Miners sent to Merrickville to maintain order during the construction period. On the canal cut above the upper lock, a steamboat can be seen docking beside a small gable-roofed structure, the first warehouse erected in Merrickville to take advantage of the transport facilities provided by the new canal.

The canal was a real boon to Merrickville especially since, in contrast to a number of other mill sites on the canal route, the mill complex there was not demolished or otherwise rendered inoperable. Previously the high cost of land transport and the impossible water communication restricted the saw and grist mills to cutting lumber and grinding grain exclusively for local consumption. With the completion of the canal, large shipments of saw logs, flour, wheat and potash were forwarded to the Montreal export market. In passing overland to the St. Lawrence naviga-

tion, travellers had taken upwards of 20 days to reach
Montreal, but with the canal in operation, heavy bulk
freight could be forwarded there in five days by steamboat.

Maitland's Rapids, Rideau [*Kilmarnock*] *19 Augᵗ 1830*

J. P. Cockburn, watercolour, 6" × 9⁹⁄₁₆"
Royal Ontario Museum

This scene is typical of the several scattered clearings along the Rideau when work began on the canal. For the most part, settlements consisted of a single-family dwelling and one or two outbuildings. The rough-hewn squared-log house, with a single door and window, appears to have a roof of wide boards, perhaps purchased at the Merrickville sawmill. The shanty, with the single door and sloped roof of interlocking split and hollowed logs — a trough or scoop roof — was probably the first building erected on the site. Owning to a scarcity of draught animals, the relatively recent date of settlement and the lack of any efficient transport system to provide access to markets, little land was cleared in the Rideau interior. Settlers lived by subsistence farming, growing wheat, corn and the dietary staple, potatoes.

Despite the rich soil bordering the Rideau River, settlers were slow to move into the region and it was only in the 1790s that Loyalists and others established small settlements on the Rideau River and Irish Creek. In 1793 the Deputy Surveyor of Upper Canada, John Stegmann, surveyed four new townships in the wilderness of the lower Rideau River between the south branch of the Rideau (Kemptville Creek) and the Ottawa River, and by the turn of the century the sons and daughters of the Loyalists were being granted lands in Nepean, Gloucester, North Gower and Osgoode townships; however, few actually settled on the Rideau.

When the Smyth Commission submitted its report in September 1825, it was assumed that Upper Canada would provide the land for the Rideau Canal free of charge in exchange for the benefits such a canal would yield the province. If the province did not prove that generous, it was hoped the lands could be bought before the project became known and inflated land prices. However, the canal was undertaken so quickly that nothing could be done beforehand to acquire the land.

By was able to secure land along the lower Rideau but difficulties developed in identifying and contacting absentee landowners on the canal route farther inland. By approached the Lieutenant Governor of Upper Canada, Sir Peregrine Maitland, who secured in February 1827 the passage of the Rideau Canal Act which gave By authority to expropriate all lands required for the construction of the canal. The amount of compensation to be paid would be settled by arbitration following the canal's construction.

In the interim, By attempted to purchase as much land as he could at reasonable prices for the canal and for defence purposes. In each case, the agreed purchase price and a survey of the land was forwarded to the Earl of Dalhousie for final approval. However, purchases were delayed by the exorbitant demands of landowners and the limitations of the act, which did not authorize the expropriation of lands for military purposes. As well, it was expensive and time consuming in many cases to determine the exact extent of the lands to be drowned by the canal.

In an effort to obtain the land required, By adopted a lease-back system apparently of his own devising. If a landowner agreed to a moderate price per acre, By purchased the whole of the property and leased it back to the former owner for 30 years at an annual rent of five per cent of the total purchase price. Although the government ended up buying far more land than it needed, inflating By's expenditures well beyond his original estimate, the price obtained was reasonable.

Moreover, in By's estimation, the lease-back system saved the Ordnance upwards of half of what otherwise

might have had eventually to be paid in damage claims. Had the lessees paid their rent and had the British government not forced the Ordnance to transfer their lands to the province in 1856, the rents alone would have yielded a 50-per-cent profit over the term of the leases.

Maitland's Rapids; 1832

John Burrows, pencil sketch, 4½" × 15"
Public Archives of Canada, C-11166

The lock at Maitland's Rapids was constructed in a 450-yard-long cut across a major bend in the river. To flood the shallow rapids in the river bend, a five-foot-high timber brace/stop-log dam was anchored to the river bedrock. A 400-yard embankment was built across the low-lying land between the head of the lock and the dam. The canal cut and lock are in the foreground of the sketch. The wooden dam can be seen at the far end of the long embankment, on the other side of the island formed by the canal excavation.

A wooden waste weir (not shown) was also erected in the embankment a short distance from the lock. The two buildings on the far side of the river belonged to a Mr. Maitland, who settled on the site several years before the canal was constructed. Maitland's Rapids marked the beginning of the "Upper Rideau Settlement," which consisted of small clearings scattered along the banks of the upper Rideau River, where the land was relatively fertile and heavily timbered.

The history of construction at Maitland's is a good example of the difficulties that plagued By and the contractors all along the system. Initially the work seemed straightforward, but once the land was cleared and excavation began, a number of problems appeared. First of all, a low-lying swamp was discovered in the river bend and the upstream riverbanks were too low to hold the higher water level. Then the soft mud of the canal cut turned out to be full of huge boulders and the excavation gave off a nauseous odour of decayed vegetable matter. When malaria struck in August 1828, the workers blamed the foul air and refused to continue digging.

To solve these problems, By lowered the height of the dam, as well as the lock lift, by two feet and built the embankment seen in the sketch. The river channel was deepened upstream to make it a navigable depth. The direction of the canal cut was changed, forcing the contractor to excavate through solid rock instead of soft mud. All of these changes increased the cost of the works at Maitland's Rapids and the total figure was double what By originally estimated. Nonetheless the exceptionally low lift of the altered lock, two feet six inches, did enable savings to be effected by doing away with the masonry breastwork in favour of anchoring wooden sills to the rock floor, and further savings were made by constructing the river dam and waste weir of wood.

In 1832 a rolling bridge was erected across the lock and during the 1840s a defensible lockmaster's house was built on a knoll a short distance from the lock. Today the lock and embankment remain as originally constructed, but a second storey has been added to the lockmaster's house. The waste weir and dam have long since been reconstructed in concrete, and a timber swing bridge has replaced the original bridge over the lock.

Maitlands Rapids
1839

93

Edmon's; 1832

John Burrows, pencil sketch, 6½" × 9½"
Public Archives of Canada, C-11167

At Edmunds Rapids, three and a half miles above the Maitland's locksite, a small rocky island divided the Rideau River into two shallow channels strewn with boulders. Over the years the locksite has been variously referred to as Edmond's, Edmon's, and Edmunds. The two dwellings below the dam belong to one of the first settlers in the area, James Edmunds, whose clearing bordered the river. The buildings on the far bank above the dam housed canal workers during the construction period. On the near bank are several additional canal buildings.

In his initial layout of the canal works between Maitlands and Old Sly's, By had planned to construct a lock and dam at each of two intermediate sites: Edmunds Rapids and Phillip's Bay. However, once the land was cleared and re-surveyed, the total difference of elevation to be surmounted turned out to be two feet less than originally recorded and the riverbanks above Edmunds Rapids proved higher than first reported. By was able to eliminate the works at Phillip's Bay in favour of raising the waters at Edmunds and deepening the river slightly below Old Sly's to obtain a navigable depth between them.

The lock at Edmunds has a lift of eight feet eight inches and the overflow dam is 13 feet high. A long earth embankment was raised along the bank beside the canal cut and a masonry waste weir was installed. Two noteworthy steps were taken to economize on the cost of the site. To avoid the expense of clay puddle, gravel and broken stone from the nearby quarry were packed in front of the stone keywork of the dam, as was done successfully at Clowes Quarry. However, the puddle wall in the earth embankment was retained. Further savings were made by substituting a wooden floor, built of heavy hemlock sleepers covered with planking, for the masonry floor customary in locks on clay foundations. Wood kept continuously under water was considered to be as durable as stone, and it could be procured and worked more cheaply.

Today the overflow dam, waste weir and lock at Edmunds remain virtually as constructed, but the wooden buildings have long since disappeared. The Edmunds and Clowes Quarry overflow dams remain the best examples of the stone arched overflow dam that By originally intended to contruct at all of the locksites on the canal.

Edmons
1832

95

Old Sly's Locks; ca. 1840s

John Burrows, watercolour over pencil, 9" × 12½"
Archives of Ontario

Two combined locks with a total lift of 16 feet 6 inches were constructed at Old Sly's in a canal cut in the left bank of the river. A 23-foot-high dam was built across the river channel to flood the rapids and back up a stillwater of navigable depth to Smiths Falls, a mile upstream. A defensible lockmaster's house, erected in 1838, can be seen beside the upper lock; to its right is a lock labourer's house and a shed.

The first settler on this site was William Sly, who arrived with his family in 1798 and by 1824 had erected a substantial barn and house where the defensible lockmaster's house was later constructed. By the 1840s, the area surrounding the locksite was mostly cleared farmland and within a decade two mills were erected by a local entrepreneur, Joshua Bates. A store, owned by a Mr. Matheson, and a wharf were constructed at the lockstation just upstream of the lockmaster's house. The building shown may well be Matheson's store.

When the Kempt Committee decided that the locks were to be enlarged, the alignment of the Old Sly's locks had to be altered slightly. They had been laid out at an angle, with the lower lock pointing out into the centre of the river below the dam, to save rock excavation by shortening the canal cut, but whereas the sharp angle of entry was no problem for gunboats, it was considered too difficult, if not impossible, for the longer steamboats. Hence the locks were altered to run parallel to the river and the cut was carried farther downstream to make a straight entry into the river.

Another change was made in 1829 in response to By's decision to construct waste weirs to protect the Rideau dams. The dam at Old Sly's had to be raised to prevent water from flowing over it. The coping of the dam was opened and raised three feet to match the height of the upper lock wall. To control the water level, a wooden waste weir was constructed in a 60-foot-wide channel (on the left of the drawing) cut to divert the river water while work proceeded on the dam and locks.

The only other alteration was of a minor nature, but unique to Old Sly's. The lower lock was constructed with a bare rock floor as planned, but blasting in the upper lockpit fractured the bedrock. To render the chamber watertight, a partial wooden floor had to be set on cross members anchored to the bedrock. On the whole canal this was the only wooden floor laid over bedrock.

Over the years the appearance of the Old Sly's lockstation has been altered dramatically. In 1857 a road crossing was opened when Bates erected a wooden swing bridge — the only privately owned bridge on the canal — over the upper lock and a fixed bridge over the waste weir to provide access to his new mills. The next year, the Brockville and Ottawa Railway completed an embankment and high-level bridge across the river and canal cut just below the locks.

In 1960, after the mills had long since disappeared, a new concrete waste weir and fixed bridge were built and the roadway was further improved with the erection of a steel swing bridge over the upper lock in 1962. In the 1960s a land fill between the railway embankment and the roadway totally obscured the stone arched dam and the original course of the river.

The defensible lockmaster's house was stripped down to its stone walls in 1965 and reconstructed as a modern lock office that bears little resemblance to its original function. Today only the lock masonry remains as originally built, and much of the ashlar (dressed stone) facing on

the outside of the exposed walls has been covered by the
land fill.

Near old Sly's, Rideau; August 1830

J. P. Cockburn, watercolour, pen and ink, 10½" × 14⅝"
Public Archives of Canada, C-12607

The size of the oak trees that were cut and rafted down the Rideau each spring can be judged by the immense stumps in this scene. The axeman is dressed in the fashion of the French Canadians employed on the canal. They generally wore a toque, shirt, trousers and moccasins, supplemented in winter by mittens and a capote (hooded blanket coat). By the late 1820s as many as 2000 French Canadians were employed in the Ottawa Valley timber trade and with the onset of a timber depression in 1826-27, large numbers of these skilled lumbermen obtained employment with the Rideau contractors as axemen, ox-drivers and labourers.

Artisans and labourers on the Rideau project were expected to provide their own tools, the contractors being responsible for housing and feeding their employees during the work season. Workers who did not possess tools had to purchase them from the contractors, who received spades, picks and shovels from the Commissariat Department at cost.

This bush, or bridle, path through the woods was cut after 1818 to connect the new military settlement at Richmond with the Rideau Lakes. It ran from Richmond directly to the Rideau River, followed the near bank of the river through the Lower Rideau Settlement — Burritts Rapids, Nicholsons and Merrick's Mills — and continued past the Upper Rideau Settlement to the outlet of the Rideau Lakes just above First Rapids (Poonamalie). The path was typical of those cut through the woods to the isolated locksites to provide a route along which quarry stone and heavy timber were hauled by yokes of oxen.

Massive amounts of supplies also had to be transported along these paths. Fodder for the draught animals could be purchased from the settlers scattered along the canal route, but most of the food for the workers was transported inland from Hull Township, the St. Lawrence or the United States. This included beef, pork, flour, potatoes, dried peas, beans and corn, tea, sugar and salt, as well as the whiskey and tobacco sold to the workers in the contractors' stores.

The lower Rideau was supplied by a 24-mile road cut through the woods in 1827 from Bytown to the navigable water above the Long Island Rapids. From there cargo was forwarded by water. On the Cataraqui a wagon road extended from Kingston through Upper Brewers Mills to the locksites along the upper reaches of the river.

Locksites in the central portion of the waterway were supplied from the St. Lawrence front via two routes to the interior. The Brockville Road connected Brockville to the Rideau Lakes, with a branch running on to Perth. It was used extensively, though like most settlement roads it was cluttered with stumps and rocks and blocked by large bogs. In the wet seasons the road might be impassable for weeks on end but in winter sleds easily pulled heavy loads along the snow-covered surface. At that time of year teamsters worked at a frantic pace to move quarried stone and provisions to the locksites. The second supply route from the St. Lawrence was the Prescott Trail that ran from Prescott to the Rideau near Burritts Rapids but it was little better than a walking path through the woods.

Smith's Falls; ca. 1845

John Burrows, watercolour over pencil, 9" × 12½"
Archives of Ontario

At the beginning of the canal project, Smiths Falls, about a mile above Old Sly's, was an isolated mill site in the midst of wilderness. The land was granted as early as 1786 to a Loyalist, Major Thomas Smyth, but was left unattended until 1823 when he erected a sawmill and dam there. Two years later, the mill was purchased by a New Yorker, Abel Russell Ward, who erected a log house and put the mill in operation.

The canal, however, was responsible for the first real settlement at Smiths Falls. In 1827 a Mr. Rykert and James Simpson, an Irish engineer from New York State, received the contract for the canal works at Smiths Falls. Rykert opened a store near Ward's house and erected four or five buildings to house the canal workers. During the canal construction period, Ward's sawmill had to be removed to make way for the dam, but he constructed a new sawmill and a flour mill on the waste water channel. Simpson, the contractor, built a grist mill just below the dam and constructed roads through the bush to Merrick's Mills and the Brockville Road, and a small village sprang up on that bank of the river.

At Smiths Falls, the Rideau River fell almost 36 feet in less than a quarter mile through the limestone rock of the Precambrian Shield which extended southward across the Rideau Lakes area. The rock was so hard that it almost defied removal by blasting, and it was full of fissures and springs. These factors, plus the fear that the low riverbanks would be flooded when the water was raised, forced By to change his original plans for the site. Three combined locks, with a lift of 25 feet, were located in a short canal excavation across the sharp bend in the river. The locks raised the canal into a basin formed by two long embankments.

The stone arched dam (seen at the far right of the painting) was built 23 feet high to prevent water flowing over it, and a waste weir was constructed across the snye channel on the right side of the basin. To flood the shallow rapids on both sides of the island above the basin, an additional, detached lock of eight-and-one-half-foot lift was built in one channel and a wooden waste weir of four-foot height in the other. The works backed up the river at a navigable depth to First Rapids, two and a half miles upstream at the outlet of the Rideau Lakes.

All of the canal structures were set on solid rock, the locks having bare rock floors. However, fissures in the rock floor of the five-and-a-half-foot deep canal basin and in the bedrock at the dam caused serious leakage that could not be overcome. Water continued to escape from the basin or flow past the dam (as indicated in the watercolour) despite all efforts to stop it.

By the mid-1840s, when the watercolour was painted, there was a defensible lockmaster's house at both the detached and the combined locks, as well as separate lock labourers' houses, and the land surrounding the locksite was cleared and settled. A number of private buildings had also been built on the island between the locks and the waste-weir channel. These included two stores, four or five dwellings, a blacksmith's shop, a granery, several stables, a tannery and, directly on the waste-weir channel, a sawmill and a grist mill. Another flour mill (not shown) was located on the opposite side of the waste channel just below the dam, as well as a number of stores. The village of Smiths Falls (not shown), sometimes called Wardville, was situated at the end of the fixed bridge over the river channel. A rolling bridge carried the road over the lower locks.

Smiths Falls grew rapidly in the early post-canal construction period, when potash and flour were shipped in large quantities to Montreal by the canal. By 1845 the village had a population of 700 and by 1850 there were over 200 houses as well as a growing number of mills, factories and commercial businesses. By mid-century, Smiths Falls had surpassed both Merrickville and Kemptville, on the south branch of the Rideau River, as the major village in the Rideau interior.

Today, the general configuration of the canal at Smiths Falls remains approximately as it was. The waste weirs have been renewed in concrete and the canal basin lined with concrete walls, but all four locks and the stone arched dam are still in place. In 1959 a concrete retaining wall was constructed upstream of the dam in an attempt to end the leakage problem and earth was dumped on both sides of the stone dam, almost obliterating it.

A large concrete lock of 26-foot lift was also built to the right of the combined locks in 1972-73, at which time a new bridge crossing was constucted. The new lock is hydraulically operated in contrast to the combined locks and the detached lock, which are still manually operated. The defensible lockmaster's house at the detached lock was demolished in 1895, but the other at the combined locks survives, although during the 1920s a second storey was added to it to provide better accommodation for the lockmaster.

First Rapids [*Poonamalie*]; ca. 1845

John Burrows, watercolour, 9" × 12½"
Archives of Ontario

First Rapids, as the name implies, was the first set of rapids on the Rideau River at the outlet of the Rideau Lakes, about three miles above Smiths Falls. It proved to be one of the most difficult of the minor rapids to surmount because of the nature of the terrain. To overcome shallow rapids, a canal engineer could adopt one of three basic approaches: a high dam at the base of the rapids could raise the water, the rapids could be excavated to a navigable depth, or a canal cut could bypass the rapids.

At First Rapids, all three had drawbacks. The riverbanks were too low to permit the waters to be raised the necessary 12 to 15 feet and the surrounding country and riverbed were of a hard limestone that could not be easily excavated. Initially, By had planned to construct a canal cut on the west bank of the river where the land was low and rock excavation could be saved by embanking. A contract was let in February 1828 to two Perth merchant-entrepreneurs, Ferguson and Wylie, to construct a low stone arched dam across the river, excavate a canal cut, and build a lock.

However, once the land was cleared and resurveyed, it was found that the original levels were incorrect, which would mean much more embanking than previously calculated in an area where little earth and virtually no clay suitable for making puddle was found. The rock in the base of the shallow cut also turned out to be of an open-layered nature which would be difficult to render watertight.

To overcome these difficulties, By relocated the canal cut to the opposite bank of the river where it could be dug through clay and loose stone on a slightly longer (one and a half miles) routing. To further minimize excavation work, the lock, of six-foot four-inch lift, was relocated from its original position at the bottom end of the cut to the mid-section to take advantage of the lay of the land, and was given a wooden floor. (In the drawing the river can be seen in the foreground, and the mid-section of the cut leading toward the Rideau Lakes, on the horizon.) The dam had masonry abutments and was 365 feet long and four feet high. The dam and lock raised the water in the river above to the 276-foot level of the Rideau Lakes, the original summit level of the canal.

While the canal was under construction, a sizeable trade developed with the Perth merchants and farmers of the surrounding district who supplied the contractors on the upper Rideau sites with pork, potatoes and other produce to feed the canal workers. This trade brought money into circulation in Perth and marked the first time that an extensive trade was carried on by way of the Tay River. Until then, Perth's commercial dealings were carried out for the most part by barter and its trade overland with Brockville.

The two buildings to the far left of the painting are all that remained circa 1845 of the eight or nine log buildings erected there to serve as a work camp during the construction of the canal. The structure close to the lock is a defensible lockmaster's house erected in the early 1840s. Little settlement took place in the area for there was only a thin layer of soil over bedrock.

Today First Rapids, renamed Poonamalie later in the 19th century, remains relatively isolated. The canal cut, lock and defensible lockmaster's house are almost as built, but a concrete overflow dam is now located on the site of the former wooden one.

103

Rideau Canal — Lock No. 32 [First Rapids]; 1854

Edwin Whitefield, watercolour on pencil, 5½" × 9½"
Public Archives of Canada, C-13299

Originally By planned that lockmasters' houses would be separate from any military structures defending the canal. He offered to pay half the cost of building a rubble-stone house at each locksite if the contractor would absorb the other half in return for its use during work at the site. Only two contractors agreed to do so; stone lockmasters' houses were erected by Phillips and White at Black Rapids and Long Island, and by Robert Drummond at Kingston Mills. Elsewhere contractors preferred to throw up log shanties to house their workers.

The possibility of constructing defensible lockmasters' houses to serve the dual functions of accommodation and defence was first raised by the Kempt Committee, but thereafter By decided to build a fortified depot at Bytown and 22 blockhouses, one at each locksite. Blockhouses would defend the canal and house the lockmaster and lock labourers in peacetime. However, only four were completed before financial restraints ended that plan.

In the aftermath of the 1837 rebellion, it became apparent that American-based raiders might try to blow up the works at isolated locksites. To strengthen the defences provided by the existing blockhouses, log guardhouses were built at Jones Falls and the White Fish dam, and defensible lockmasters' houses at Old Sly's, Clowes and Nicholsons.

During the 1840s, defensible lockmasters' houses were built at the 13 remaining locksites lacking defences. All were single-storey buildings with thick rubble masonry walls and heavy timber roofs covered in tin. Most had loopholes in the walls, but several had loopholes only in the heavy wooden shutters that closed over the windows. The structures were sited to provide a covering fire for the canal structures and were intended to withstand the musketry of small bands of marauders unaccompanied by artillery.

Defensible lockmasters' houses appear to have been unique to the Rideau Canal. Today, 12 still stand, including this one at Poonamalie. A number had second storeys added or were clapboarded during the late 19th century so that their military purpose is not always evident.

104

Rideau Canal — Lock No 32.

Perth, the Capital of the District of Dalhousie; from the N. East bank of the River Tay; sketched 20th August 1828

Thomas Burrowes, watercolour, 6½" × 10⅝"
Archives of Ontario

In June 1816 Cockburn Island in the Pike (Tay) River was selected as the site for the first military settlement in the Rideau interior. The village was laid out on either side of the island, which was a Crown reserve. A stores depot (on the right) was erected on the island to dispense provisions and tools to the settlers, and in the following year two bridges were built to connect both sections of the village.

Among the first settlers were 700 persons from Perth, Scotland, who came under the assisted emigration scheme. They were followed by veterans from the 100th Regiment of Foot, the Glengarry Light Infantry Regiment of Fencibles, the Canadian Fencibles, and the De Watteville Regiment. By 1817, over 1000 soldiers had settled in the area and Irish immigrants began to arrive in growing numbers.

During the early years, the settlers could grow barely enough for their own requirements and were heavily dependent on Commissariat rations for survival. Only in 1823 did the wheat crop yield a surplus for sale. Heavy transportation costs led Perth merchants to investigate the practicability of building a bateaux system via the Tay and Rideau Rivers down the Ottawa River to the export markets of Lower Canada. Lack of capital frustrated this plan, but with the start of the Rideau project in 1826, the Perth merchants sought to establish a link with it via the Tay.

The Tay Navigation Company was incorporated in 1831 and construction began on the Tay Canal in June 1831 when a contract was let for the first two locks at Barbadoes (Port Elmsley), about a mile and half up the Tay from the Rideau Lakes. Little work was completed in 1832 because of a lack of funds, malaria and heavy rains. The next year, however, construction proceeded quickly. The completed canal was ten miles long and included five separate locks, six dams, two swing bridges and a turning basin in Perth.

Following the canal's opening at the start of the 1834 navigation season, the company erected a wharf and warehouse at Barbadoes where freight barges towed by a steam tug were exchanged with the Rideau Canal steamboats. Owing to a lack of capital and heavy construction debt, the company was never able to properly maintain its canal, which gradually silted up. Since the Tay Canal was then too shallow for the tug, barges were poled and towed from the banks. After 1849 the canal was used only by merchants floating squared timber and saw logs to the Rideau Lakes for export.

When the federal Department of Railways and Canals reconstructed the Tay Canal in 1885-91, it was built on an altered course from Beveridge Bay, on the Rideau Lakes, directly to the upper Tay River. This route not only shortened the canal by several miles, but also eliminated many of the structures required on the old route. Two masonry locks were constructed at Beveridges. Each had a chamber 33 by 134 feet to match the Rideau locks and a 13-foot lift. A low overflow dam was constructed across the Tay just below its junction with the canal cut to raise the water in the upper river.

Today, the Beveridge Locks and Tay Canal are operated as part of the Rideau system. Several embankments of the old Tay Canal can still be seen on the lower Tay River near Port Elmsley, but the timber-crib overflow dams and wooden locks have long since rotted away.

Lock, Blockhouse &c at the Narrows, Rideau Lake — the first descent from Summit towards Bytown; 1841

Thomas Burrowes, watercolour, 6¼" × 9¼"
Archives of Ontario

Nineteen and a half miles above First Rapids and 80 miles from the Ottawa River, a long tongue of land protruded across the Rideau Lakes to within 100 feet of the south shore. The water at the Narrows was very shallow and initially By planned merely to deepen the channel and maintain a 33-mile-long summit reservoir stretching from First Rapids across the Rideau Lakes through a canal cut at the Isthmus and across the lakes on the upper Cataraqui River to Chaffeys Mills. However, excavation at the Isthmus was much more difficult than expected and By sought ways to reduce the amount of work required.

When it was determined that the upper part of the Rideau Lakes could be raised about five feet without overflowing its rocky margins, By decided to raise it four feet ten inches by constructing canal works at the Narrows. In effect, the summit of the waterway was to be raised to the 281-foot level and the size of the reservoir drastically reduced to save a corresponding four-foot ten-inch depth of rock excavation on the Isthmus cut. This required a lock and weir at the Narrows, as well as a straight earth and clay dam and an embankment along the south shore. They divided the Rideau Lakes into two levels: Upper Rideau Lake and, on the lower level, Big Rideau Lake and Lower Rideau Lake.

The two-storey blockhouse was built in 1832-33. It was roofed with cedar shingles and may have been surrounded by a moat of water. Access was provided only at the second-storey level by the stairway to the embankment. The long walkway to the lock was added in 1836. The Narrows blockhouse could accommodate a garrison of 20 men, but in peacetime housed the lockmaster and lock labourers. The function of the two sheds in front of the blockhouse is unknown. The wooden waste weir was located a short distance to the right of the blockhouse.

Over the years, the embankment at the Narrows has been widened slightly and the waste weir has been rebuilt in concrete. The lock remains as constructed, but the blockhouse was restored in 1967-70. The land around the blockhouse was raised three feet to the level of the dam, and a door was cut through the renewed masonry wall of the lower storey to provide access to a public washroom installed within. The only other major change at the site was the erection of a wooden swing bridge over the lock chamber in 1867 to provide a road connection across the Narrows dam. That bridge was replaced in 1964 by a manually operated, steel truss swing bridge.

109

Upper Rideau Lake; — Canoe en route to Bytown; — Westport in the distance; post-1832

Thomas Burrowes, watercolour, 6¼" × 9¼"
Archives of Ontario

Birchbark canoes of the large, 36-foot, *canot de maitre* (or Montreal canoe) type were used by the fur brigades on the main fur trade route to the west up the Ottawa River and across the Mattawa/French rivers and the upper Great Lakes to Fort William. Because of their shallow draft these canoes were a favoured means of transportation on the Rideau system during canal construction. They were used first in the spring of 1827 when By hired six Hudson's Bay Company canoes and their crews to carry himself, some of his staff and several interested contractors through the route Clowes proposed. By hoped to award on the spot any contracts for which he received moderate bids. He had calculated that it would take three weeks to reach Kingston, but once under way, the voyageurs set the pace: it took three days.

On the fur brigades the voyageurs were accustomed to setting out as early as four o'clock in the morning and paddling until dusk with only intermittent stops for a brief smoke or bite to eat. By dint of incessant paddling, quickened by tots of rum and periodic singing, they were able to cover great distances very rapidly. On the Rideau trip, each potential locksite was examined, the longest stops being for 1½ hours at the foot of Long Island and 2¼ hours at Jones Falls, and yet the flotilla still covered 33 miles the first day, 52 miles the second, and 29 miles on the third day to arrive at Kingston about nine o'clock that evening. By's first trip through the Rideau system was consequently exceptionally short but extremely productive even though no major contracts were let.

The painting shows Thomas Burrowes and his assistants being paddled across Upper Rideau Lake by French-Canadian voyageurs in their traditional dress. The stone channel marker with its upright pole is the type originally constructed at the approach to locksites on the canal.

Dam at Jones' Falls; when nearly completed, showing the last temporary passage provided for the surplus water; 1831

Thomas Burrowes, watercolour, 6¼" × 10½"
Archives of Ontario

Engineering the Canal

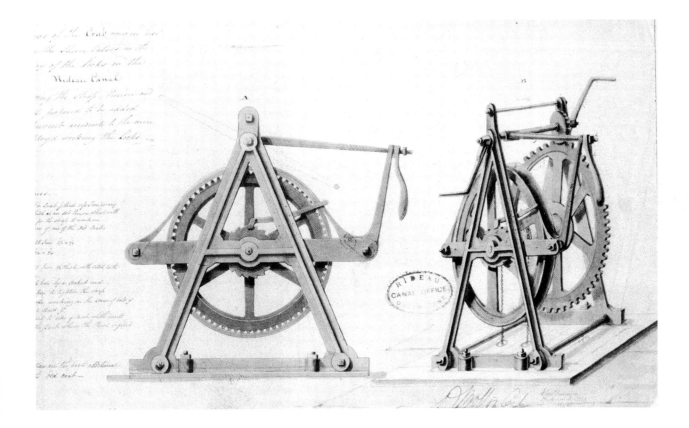

Rideau Canal [The Isthmus, later Newboro]; ca. 1832

John Burrows, pencil sketch
Public Archives of Canada, C-18798

Locks are basically hydraulic machines which lift and lower boats by the principle of gravity: when released, a confined body of water will always flow into a lower level of water to attain a common level. Each lock consists of a watertight chamber — usually rectangular to accommodate conventional boats — with gates at either end and sluice valves to control the flow of water in and out of the chamber.

To pass up through the lock, a boat enters the chamber through the open lower gates. The gates are closed, the upper sluices opened, and the water above the lock flows through the open sluices into the lock until the water in the chamber and the boat floating on it reach the level of the canal above. With water pressure on either side of the gates now equal, the upper gates are easily cranked open and the boat moves out into the upper reach of the canal to continue its journey.

To pass down through the lock, a boat enters the chamber through the open upper gates. The upper gates and sluice valves are then closed and the lower sluice valves opened, allowing water in the lock chamber to flow out into the lower level of the canal. Once the water level and boat in the lock chamber have dropped to the lower level, the flow of water out of the chamber ceases. The lock operator cranks open the lower gates and the boat may leave the lock. The next upstream-bound boat is then able to enter and start the process over again. On the Rideau each lockage took about 12 minutes. Unladen small craft, such as the canoe in this sketch, were simply portaged around the lock.

The masonry chamber and operating mechanisms of the Isthmus lock, shown in the sketch, are typical of the Rideau locks. The crabs, a type of winch, on the lock walls opened and closed the lock gates by means of an endless chain that passed down the wall and across the floor of the lock to the base of each gate and back. The rack and pinion mechanisms on the top of the gates operated the sluice valves at the bottom of each gate, the standard location for sluices on the lower gates of locks. Most upper sluice valves were placed in tunnels passing through the lock wall, though, as the sketch shows, at the Isthmus the upper sluices were in the gates.

The Isthmus lock overcame an eight-foot difference between the level of the water in the canal cut extension of Upper Rideau Lake and the level of the Mud Lake headwaters of the Cataraqui River. The difference in elevation to be overcome in carrying a canal from one level of water to the next determined the number of locks required at each locksite. Each lock was generally given a "lift" or "fall" of from five to ten feet.

Where large differences of elevation were to be overcome, a number of locks were combined, with the total lift or fall evenly divided among them. Most of the Rideau locks had lifts from eight to ten feet; however, it proved necessary to construct a few locks with either exceptionally low or exceptionally high lifts because of the nature of the ground at a particular locksite. For example, the lift at Maitland's was two feet three inches and at Jones Falls were 15 feet on each lock.

On the Rideau Canal, 47 masonry locks were constructed at 22 locksites to overcome a total difference of elevation of 444 feet 7 inches: 33 locks raised the canal 281 feet 2 inches from the Ottawa River to Upper Rideau Lake, and 14 locks descended 163 feet 5 inches from Upper Rideau Lake to Lake Ontario. All of the locks were built with a minimum of six feet of water on the sills to allow for fluctuations in the water level.

Plan and Section of a Single Lock for the Rideau Canal as Approved by Committee of which Sir J. Kempt was president; ca. 1828

Col. John By, R.E.
Public Record Office

This basic plan was adopted for the Rideau locks. It called for lock chambers (a) 33 feet wide by 134 feet long sill-to-sill to leave an 110-foot clearance when the lower gates were swung open. The masonry walls were to be eight feet thick at the base and five feet thick at the coping, or top of the wall, with a batter, or slope, on the inner face in the lock chamber. The rear of each wall was reinforced by four-foot-square counterfort piers (b) on roughly 20-foot centres. Each wall was thickened adjacent to the lower gates to enable it to withstand the force of the water thrusting the gates back against the hollow quoin pier (c) in which each gate pivoted.

Lock walls were also thickened at the upper gates where tunnel sluices (d) were to pass in and down through the walls to fill the lock and manholes (e) were to provide access to the tunnels. The sluices for emptying the lock were placed in the lower gates. Walls were to be made of rubble stone masonry with a dressed stone (ashlar) facing of blocks up to 20 inches wide and from 3½ to 5½ feet long by 18 to 24 inches high. The stones were laid alternately header and stretcher with the headers tying in with the rubble masonry backing.

The locks adopted for the Rideau Canal were of a standard design, although much larger than most contemporary ones. At the upper end of the lock, a breastwork (f) was to step down from the upper navigation level to the lower.

Where the lock was constructed in clay or earth, a row of sheet piling (g) was to be driven across the lock behind the breastwork and below the lock floor to prevent water from penetrating under the floor. In clay or earth, an inverted arch of stone masonry would floor the lock chamber, whereas in solid bedrock, the floors were the natural rock.

The pointed masonry sill (h) against which the upper gates closed was built on the breastwall, and the sill for the lower gates (i) was built on the lockpit floor. As a cost-saving measure, By adopted the common practice of building the lower sill and gate-recess (j) floor of wood, as shown here. Wooden sills were also placed at the base of the stop-log grooves (k) in the upper and lower wing walls (l) so the lock could be dammed and pumped dry for repairs.

To prevent ground water seeping into the lock masonry, a two-foot-thick wall of clay puddle (m) was built up against the outside of the lock walls prior to backfilling the lockpit.

Puddled clay was used to render canal beds and banks watertight where cuts had to be taken through any permeable ground. Unworked clay was not impervious to water, but if mixed with coarse sand or fine gravel, wetted and chopped, beaten and kneaded, it could be so consolidated as to be completely watertight if used where it could be kept wet. When properly worked, it condensed to approximately two-thirds of its original bulk.

Like other material required on the canal, the cost of puddling was higher than By anticipated. In many instances puddle clay could only be obtained some distance from the worksites, and he had to pay much more than his initial estimate.

116

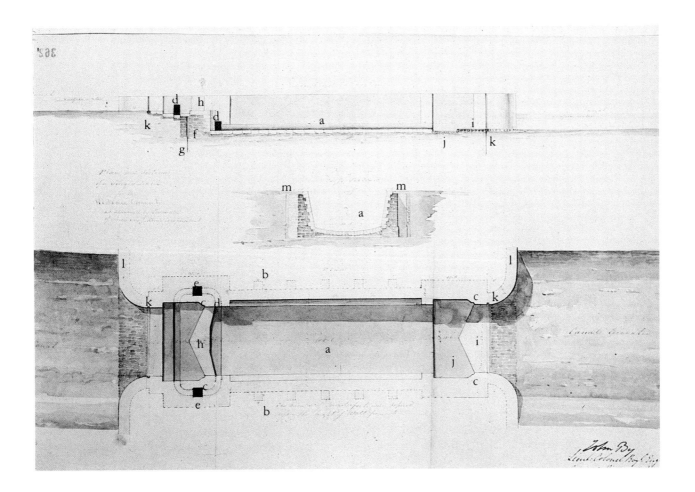

Section on line A B of a Pointed Cill [sic] and Recess as approved of by the Committee of which Sir James Kempt was president; ca. 1828

Col. John By, R.E.
Public Record Office

This section along the centre of a lock shows the original plan for the breastwork on which the upper sill of the single locks and, as shown here, the intermediate sill of combined locks rested. The breastwork was to consist of two solid units of rubble stone masonry, laid in common mortar, divided by a clay puddle wall (a) with a row of sheet piling (b) driven down through the puddle wall.

The piling was to prevent water forcing its way down through the breastwork from the upper lock chamber. The pointed cut-stone sill (c), ten feet wide from its base to its tip, was laid on top of the breastwork masonry with its tip in line with the near edge of the puddle wall.

To provide a ledge against which the closed gates could press, the sill projected one and a half feet above the gate recess floor (d).

Breastworks were generally equal in height to the lift of the lock. The front of the breastwork, the breastwall, was faced with dressed stone to match the lock chamber walls and, like the side walls, the breastwall stones (e) were laid in common mortar with square joints. Also shown in the plan are the hollow quoin pier (f) and the tunnel sluice (g).

By planned breastworks of a conventional design, but problems forced its modification. The first breastworks were undertaken in the Entrance Valley locks. The labourers found it impossible to drive the sheet piles into place because the clay contained huge boulders. Since this situation recurred in most of the clay-based sites, sheet piling had to be eliminated. In its absence, By considered the puddle wall to be a liability as it broke what would otherwise be a solid unit of masonry, which he judged thick enough to be impermeable, so the puddle wall was also eliminated.

As it turned out, the modified breastworks were defective. When the Entrance Valley locks were first tested in May 1831, the pressure of the water was so great that it forced its way through the breastwork masonry and dislodged several stones from one of the breastwalls. By's engineering staff differed as to whether the fault lay in the elimination of the sheet piling and puddle wall or in the common mortar used. There was some evidence that the common mortar had not set properly in the damp lockpits and By believed that the mistake had been in not using hydraulic cement, which would harden under water. He therefore decided all of the lock stonework would be laid and grouted with hydraulic cement.

The already existing wall and floor masonry was merely grouted with hydraulic cement, but the breastwalls and masonry sills were partially taken up and relaid using the more effective cement. As well, heavy iron straps were set into the top of the sill stones parallel to the front edge of the sills, and five- to six-foot-long fox bolts were put down through the masonry to hold the stones firmly in place. This expedient proved itself when the water was raised, since no problems arose even on the exceptionally high Jones Falls lifts.

At the locksites where the breastworks and sills had not yet been started, which included most of the locks from

Burritts Rapids to Kingston Mills inclusive, the sill stones were notched into the course below, and all of the stonework was laid in hydraulic cement with joggle joints to form a solid, interlocking mass of stone then made watertight by grouting. This enabled the contractors to dispense with the long fox bolts and iron straps.

119

Plan of Pointed Cill [sic] and Recess of Combined Locks; ca. 1828

Col. John By, R.E.
Public Record Office

Here the details of an intermediate sill and breastwork of two combined locks are shown as viewed from above in a cutaway plan. On the right is the top of the rubble stone masonry of the breastwork with the proposed wall of sheet piling through the puddle wall (a).

The pointed sill (b) was laid directly on top of the breastwork. The joggle joints (c) strengthening the masonry sills are clearly visible. (Joggle joints were formed by cutting vertical V-shaped grooves in the ends of blocks of stone prior to their being laid in hydraulic cement; the joints so formed were filled with a grout of liquid hydraulic cement.)

The back of the sill and the breastwork beneath it were slightly concave to accommodate the prow or stern of the vessel in the lock chamber below. At the upper right, the ashlar facing (d), the rubble masonry backing (e) and the clay puddle wall (f) of the lock walls are shown.

In front of the sill was the gate recess area (g), over which the gates swung. The flat recess floor of dressed stone was laid partly on the breastwork masonry and partly on a masonry foundation that extended to the floor of the upper lock chamber proper. When open, each gate rested in a recess in the lock wall. The left gate recess shows the iron journal box (h), or socket, set into the masonry at the base of the hollow quoin pier to receive the pintle in the heel post of the lock gate. A truck, or roller wheel, on the bottom of the lock gate ran on the iron rail (i) anchored to the gate recess floor.

The lock gates were originally opened and closed by means of a continuous chain that passed from the crab, down the lock wall, around an arc of chain blocks (j) anchored to the gate recess floor, to the front of the gate at the base of its mitre post, and returned around the chain blocks and up the lock wall to the crab. The chain wound around the barrel of the crab several times, and then passed back down the lock wall, around the chain blocks, around a snub sheave (k) on the sill below the gate, to the back of the mitre post, and back to the crab. With this system, the gate could be opened and closed simply by cranking the crab in one direction or the other.

A one-foot-deep, three-foot-wide gutter (l) across the gate recess floor in line with the sluice tunnel (m) intake openings trapped debris that might otherwise jam under the gates. Each of the pair of sluice tunnels was three feet wide by five feet high and the base of the intake was level with the gutter floor.

The tunnel went down through the lock wall to exit at the base of the breastwall. The discharges were opposite each other to reduce turbulence as the lock was filled by having the two shooting streams of water meet head on below the water in the lock.

Sluice tunnels were used so vessels would not be flooded by water gushing into the lock chamber from the top of the breastwork, as would be the case if the sluices were in the upper gates. This was not a problem at the lower gates of a single lock or the lowest gates on a flight of locks, and the sluices were built into the bottom of these gates. Four-and-a-half-foot square manholes (n) provided access to the in-tunnel sluice valves.

The masonry floors (o) of the lock chambers can be seen below the breastwall and above the gate recess floor. Masonry floors were constructed where the stability of the ground was in doubt. In all, 16 of the 47 Rideau Canal locks had masonry floors: the locks in the Entrance Valley, at Hartwell's, the Hog's Back, and Jones Falls.

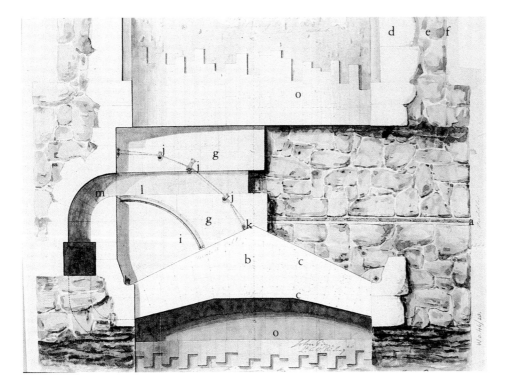

A masonry floor was usually built in the form of an inverted arch to resist upward pressure exerted by ground water penetrating under the lock chamber, and to distribute the weight and lateral pressure of the side walls more evenly, thereby preventing any partial settlement.

The two-foot-deep floor stones conformed to voussoir stones in a conventional masonry arch. They were laid on a foundation of macadamized stone built up from the lockpit floor in compacted layers of small chipped stone. Hot lime mortar was poured over each layer as it was shaped to match the curve of the arch. After the breastwork problems in the spring of 1831, immense quantities of hydraulic cement grout were forced into the masonry floors to ensure they were watertight.

121

Half Plan and Section of a Wooden pointed Sill & Apron for a Lower Gate When laid on Clay or Earth with the connexion with a wooden Floor in the Lock; ca. 1830

Col. John By, R.E.
Public Archives of Canada

The construction details of a wooden lower sill (a), gate recess floor (b) and apron, or tail bay, (c) are shown. As a cost-saving measure, the lower sills of most single locks and of the bottom lock in every flight of locks were made of wood for if kept continuously under water, as was the case with lower sills, it was considered as durable as stone. Wooden lower sills were constructed on masonry and bedrock floors from the start of the project and when By decided, again to save costs, to floor some of the locks in earth or clay with wood, the same substructure was retained below the lower sill and was connected with the wooden floor as shown.

The wooden floor in the gate recess consisted of several timbers laid in longitudinal grooves in the earth or clay of the lockpit and adzed to provide a level surface across which squared sleepers formed a solid platform. The only gap in the platform was the gate recess ditch (d). The oak sill frame was lagged to the sleepers and filled with tightly packed stone chips. Planks were set into notches in the frame and nailed flush with the top of the frame.

The plank flooring in the gate recess and ditch was nailed and notched into the sleepers to form watertight joints. Sheet piling (e) was to be driven across the base of the sill and a transverse timber placed at the base of the stop-log grooves (f) in the lock walls. The piling was to prevent water working its way into the lock chamber under the lower sill when the stop logs were in place and the lock pumped out for repair.

In the tail bay, transverse sleepers (g) were laid directly on the lockpit excavation, but with gaps between them. Here too the plank flooring was notched and nailed into the sleepers.

On lock chambers with masonry floors, the solid platform of transverse sleepers in the gate recess floor merely tightly abutted the end of the lock chamber floor, but in wood-floored locks the junction was formed as indicated in the drawing.

In the chamber proper of a wood-floored lock (h), the transverse sleepers — contrary to what is indicated in the drawing — were laid on five timbers set longitudinally into the lockpit and notched to carry the sleepers at roughly 30-inch centres. The sleepers were pinned to the timbers by heavy treenails, their tops were hewn level, and clay puddle was rammed into the gaps between them. Planks were secured across the sleepers with both wooden treenails and iron spikes.

The rubble masonry backing of the side walls was laid directly on the earth or clay of the lockpit excavation; the bottom course of the ashlar facing projected roughly one foot over the ends of the sleepers. To ensure a tight fit between the plank floor and the masonry walls, the bottom four inches of the ashlar facing was cut vertical to match the four-inch-thick planks. The planking and sleepers were generally of hemlock with occasionally oak being used.

The Rideau Canal system of wooden floors in the lower gate recess/tail bay was typical of American wood-

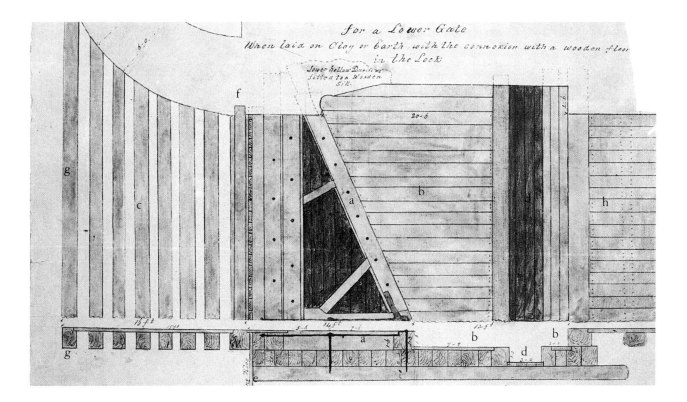

floored locks; however, in American practice, the gate recess floor was generally not stepped below the lock chamber floor but was a continuation of it. The Americans also dispensed with the gate recess ditch.

Eight of the Rideau locks had wooden floors and only the one at Lower Brewers caused serious problems. There a bad foundation continued to settle and the lock had eventually to be totally rebuilt in 1977. Tests on the sleepers removed at that time revealed that after being under water for 145 years, the wood was still sound.

The sleepers in the other wood-floored locks remain extant, although most of the plank floors have been replaced with concrete caps during the present century. Besides the original Lower Brewers lock, wooden floors were built in the single locks at Burritts Rapids, Edmunds, First Rapids and Davis; the two combined locks at Upper Brewers, and in the bottom lock at Kingston Mills.

Plan of Pointed Sill on Rock, Rideau Canal; Section on Line A B; 23 October 1840

John Burrows, pencil drawing
Public Archives of Canada

The drawing, from the post-construction period, shows a typical wooden sill on a bare rock floor. The oak sill (a) was framed and bolted in the form of a triangle, set on the levelled bedrock, anchored by fox bolts (b), and filled with random rubble masonry (c), roughly dressed and tightly jointed. A second large timber (d), was anchored 16 inches from the base of the pointed sill to form a sill at the base of the stop-log grooves (e) in the lock walls. The gap between the stop-log sill and the pointed sill was filled with clay puddle (f). Planking was inset and nailed flush with the tops of the sill frames to cover the pointed sill frame and the clay puddle gap. The gate recess floor in front of the sill was also covered with plank anchored to the bedrock.

A fox bolt was basically an iron rod with a threaded top taking a square nut, and flat iron wedge set in a groove in the bottom. When the bolt was inserted in a hole drilled in the bedrock and driven, the bottom was splayed out by the wedge, anchoring the bolt to the rock.

As building, positioning and anchoring the sill frames was very critical work, it was done by closely supervised civilian artificers employed directly by the engineering establishment. When a contractor was ready for a sill, the master carpenter, Fitzgibbon, and his men were dispatched to frame and place it.

For the most part, wooden sills were constructed only at the lower gates of locks with bare rock floors. Masonry breastworks and sills were usually constructed at the upper ends of such locks as the top of the breastwork and the upper sill were not continuously under water like lower sills.

Only four rock-floored locks had upper sills of wood and these had such exceptionally low lifts that the breastworks were eliminated. At the Narrows, the Isthmus, Maitland's and Clowes Quarry, wooden upper sills were anchored to bedrock on the same level as the lower sills and the whole height of the lift was thrown against the upper gates.

By planned bare rock floors on all locks on sound bedrock and after the first surveys he calculated that up to 30 locks could be constructed with rock floors and 17 with masonry inverts. However, bedrock was either not encountered where expected or was unsound, so the number of rock floors had to be reduced and wooden floors were substituted for masonry inverts where feasible to keep costs in line with the estimate.

Of the 47 Rideau locks, 23 had bare rock floors: the single locks at Black Rapids, Clowes Quarry, Maitland's, the Narrows, the Isthmus and Chaffeys; all of the locks at Long Island, Nicholsons, Merrickville, Old Sly's and Smiths Falls, and all but the bottom lock at Kingston Mills. At Old Sly's, the bedrock in the upper lock was badly fractured by blasting during the lockpit excavation, and in an effort to render the chamber watertight, a plank floor was built over cross timbers anchored to the rock.

With the exception of the floor of the upper lock at Old Sly's, which eventually had to be covered with a concrete slab to prevent leakage, the rock floors have lasted to the present day without any maintenance. However, a number of them are now badly fissured and there has been some undermining of the lock walls and breastwalls through wear.

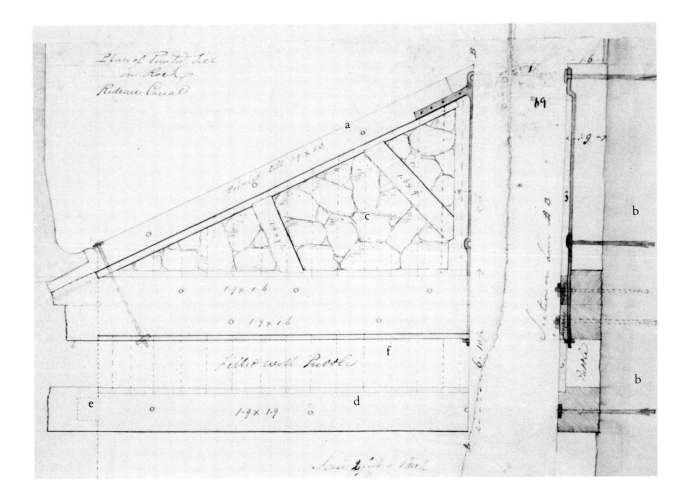

Plan of Pointed Sill
in Rock
Rideau Canal

a

c

1·9 × 1·6

1·9 × 1·6

Filled with Puddle

1·9 × 1·9

e   d   f

Scale 2 feet = 1 inch

b

b

Gate-Operating Mechanisms; 1839

Lt. William T. Denison, R.E.

"A Detailed Description of Some of the Works on the Rideau Canal," in Great Britain, Army, Corps of Royal Engineers, *Papers on Subjects Connected with the Duties of the Corps of Royal Engineers* (London: John Weale, 1839), Vol. 3, Pl. 20.

During the early 19th century, most lock gates were operated by heavy timber swing beams extending out from the top of the gate and serving not only as levers by which the gate could be opened, but also as counterweights to prevent the gate from sagging. By had initially planned to use swing bars, but when the large lock was adopted, he decided that the gates would be too large for them and adopted the crab/floor-chain system (a), with a roller wheel under the gate to keep it from sagging. The system, which may well have been of By's own devising, worked well for the first two years, but the chains tended to become fouled with debris which was difficult to clear under water.

In 1834 Captain Bolton, the superintending engineer on the Ottawa and Rideau canals, developed a curved-swing-bar/crab system (b, c). The arc of sheave blocks was relocated from the gate recess floor to the coping of the lock wall and the crab and endless chain were repositioned. The chain ran through a pin at the outer end of the swing bar, passed directly to the crab barrel, wound round the barrel several times, went around the arc of chain blocks, through a snatch or snub sheave on the wing wall of the lock, and back to the pin in the bar.

The gate could be opened by turning the crab handles in one direction to draw the bar toward the snub sheave, and closed by turning the crab handles in the opposite direction to draw the bar back towards the crab. The positioning of the swing bar on the gate itself is illustrated (c), as well as the rails added to strengthen the gates in 1832 following the initial testing of the locks in the previous year.

The conversion from the crab/floor-chain system to the curved-swing-bar/crab system began in 1835 and continued until mid-century when the curved swing bar was replaced by a straight bar along the top of the lock gate. In the late 19th century, when some of the chain blocks and sheaves were in need of replacement, a third system, the crab/push-bar system, was adopted.

In the new system, the arc of chain blocks and the sheave were eliminated in favour of a long bar of wood mounted to the top of the lock gate mitre post and passing under the crab (repositioned above the lock gates with its barrel at a right angle to the bar). The endless chain was retained: it ran from the mitre-post end of the push bar, passed directly to the crab, wound round the barrel several times, was attached to the outer end of the push bar, and returned to the crab and mitre post. Turning the crab in one direction drew the gate open and moved the bar back through the crab; turning it in the opposite direction drew the bar forward through the crab, forcing the gate closed.

The push-bar system has been gradually introduced on the Rideau locks as the chain blocks have worn out. By no means a novel system, it was introduced on the Ottawa Canals as early as 1829 by Captain DuVernet, the superintending engineer on the project, who had seen a similar system on locks in the Netherlands.

On the Rideau Canal today the original crab/floor-chain system of working the gates has been retained on one of the Entrance Valley locks and one of the Kingston Mills locks. The rest of the manually operated lock gates are worked by either the crab/swing-bar or crab/push-bar system. Hydraulically operated gates have been installed on the Black Rapids and Isthmus locks, as well as on the new high-lift lock at Smiths Falls.

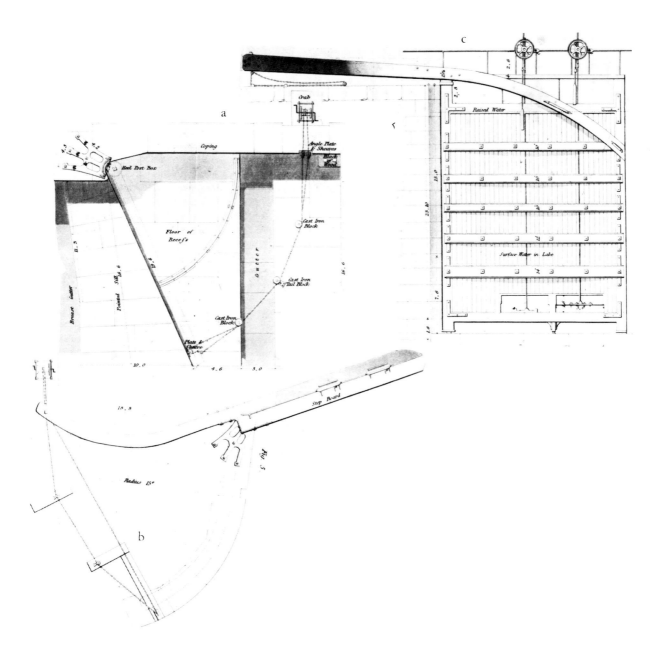

a

c

Raised Water

Surface Water in Lake

Coping

Heel Post Box

Floor of
Recess

Gutter

Angle Plate
& Sheaves
Block
Wheel

Crab

Cast Iron
Block

Cast Iron
Tail Block

Breast Gutter

Pointed Sill

Cast Iron
Block

Plate &
Sheave

10.0   4.6   3.0

Step Board

Fig. 5.

Radius 15°

b

Tunnel Sluice Valve Mechanisms; 1839

Lt. William T. Denison, R.E.

"A Detailed Description of Some of the Works on the Rideau Canal," in Great Britain, Army, Corps of Royal Engineers, *Papers on Subjects Connected with the Duties of the Corps of Royal Engineers* (London: John Weale, 1839), Vol. 3, Pl. 21.

Two distinct valve systems were initially employed on the tunnel sluices: in-tunnel sluice valves (a), which served most locks, and wall-face sluice valves (b), on locks of exceptionally high lifts such as at Jones Falls.

The in-tunnel sluice valve consisted of a flat wooden pivot plate mounted horizontally in a wooden frame in the base of the manhole shaft at the mid-point of the sluice tunnel. The valve was operated by a crab (c, d) at the top of the lock wall directly over the manhole. A chain was wound around the barrel of the crab and continued down the manhole to the valve plate. One end of the chain was attached to the bottom edge of the plate and the other end to its top edge. By cranking the crab handle in one direction, the bottom of the plate was lifted upwards, pivoting the valve open; by cranking the handle in the opposite direction, the top of the plate was pivoted back up to its closed position.

By feared that on the locks of exceptionally high lifts the in-tunnel valves might not withstand the much greater pressures to which they would be subjected, and wall-face valves were substituted at the intake ends of the sluice tunnels. Such valves were subject only to the pressure of the head of water in the lock chamber whereas the in-tunnel valves were subject to an additional pressure equal to half the height of the lift.

The wall-face valves each consisted of two iron pivot plates mounted in a wooden frame within the tunnel opening. They had horizontal axes and were positioned one above the other. Goose-neck brackets joined the plates to a connecting rod activated by a rack and pinion mechanism mounted on the edge of the lock wall coping (b, e).

Turning the crank handle in one direction raised the rod to open the valves; reversing it pushed the rod downwards, closing the valves. Where wall-face valves were originally constructed, the manhole above the sluice tunnel was eliminated in favour of a simple 14-inch-diameter air shaft up through the lock wall just behind the valves.

When the in-tunnel valves were first tested in 1830, the wooden plates were incapable of withstanding the water pressure so cast-iron plates were substituted. Several minor alterations also had to be made to strengthen the system. The wall-face valves proved equal to the pressures to which they were subjected, but often the force of the water on partially opened plates drove them closed again, spinning the crank handle.

To make the valves easier to operate and avoid injuries to the lock labourers, in 1834-35 a chain link was substituted for the rigid goose-neck bracket attaching the upper valve plate to the connecting rod. The bottom plate could then be opened partially before the slack chain began to open the upper plate, reducing the pressure experienced when both plates had acted in unison.

On the in-tunnel valves, serious injuries were caused by the force of the water driving the valve closed and spinning the crab handle out of the labourer's grasp. Efforts to put a brake on the crab proved fruitless and in 1839 all the in-tunnel valves were converted to wall-face valves. To save costs, the crabs and chains used to operate the in-tunnel valves were moved from over the manholes to the edges of the lock coping above the new wall-face valves and connected to the valves by a lift rod.

a

b

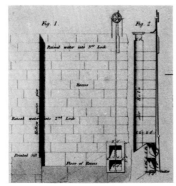

c

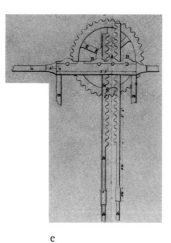

d

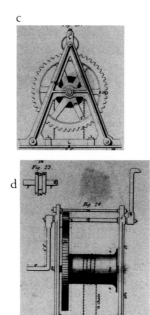

e

Today all of the sluice tunnels are operated by wall-face valves similar to those erected originally on the locks of exceptionally high lifts. The original wall-face valves are operated by rack and pinion mechanisms, and the wall-face valves of the 1839 conversion by crabs and chains.

The manholes were covered by wooden gratings in 1839, and by iron ones in 1900. Hydraulically operated valves were installed on the Black Rapids lock in 1968, and in the new high lift lock constructed at Smiths Falls in 1973-74.

129

Colonel By Watching the Building of the Rideau Canal

C. W. Jefferys, watercolour
Canadian National Hotels

Painted long after the canal was completed, the watercolour depicts By, in full dress uniform, and the contractor, Thomas McKay, at the Entrance Valley locks where Royal Sappers and Miners are working. In this artist's depiction there are several inaccuracies. The painting does not show the curved wing walls at the end of the locks, the rubble masonry behind the ashlar facing, or the header stones that tied the ashlar to the rubble masonry.

The ashlar face stone was not laid flat or level, but perpendicular to the batter, or slope, of the lock chamber wall. To bring the coping, or top, of the lock wall to a level, the coping stones were cut in a wedge shape. However, the heavy blocks of stone were indeed dressed on the locksite and laid with the aid of crabs, blocks and pulleys, and gyn poles.

Masonry contracts stated precisely how the stone was to be dressed and laid. By's overseers and engineers surveyed and laid out the work for the contractors, and established levels, wall profiles and control posts. The master mason provided templates to guide the contractors' masons in cutting and laying the stone of the sills, hollow quoins and floors, and bevels to aid them in levelling the beds of the stone off the batter of the lock walls.

Dressing the stone was critical. The beds and ends of the ashlar had to be cut square to ensure that it would be laid with tight joints and even beds to minimize settling and preventing unequal pressures from cracking any blocks. The sedimentary limestone and sandstone had to be dressed and laid to rest on its natural bed to ensure that any laminations would be at right angles to the pressure exerted on them. To lay the stone, the existing course was cleaned, moistened with water, and covered with a thin layer of mortar. A block was lowered onto the mortar, tapped firmly into place, levelled, and mortared on its end to receive the next block.

Initially, By planned to lay all of the lock stonework in common mortar and only point, or trowel, the joints with hydraulic cement. Common mortar could be made from the limestone at the locksites, but hydraulic cement had to be imported from England or the United States. In 1829 Ruggles Wright discovered near Wright's Town a type of limestone from which hydraulic cement could be made, and he began to manufacture what proved to be an excellent hydraulic cement. The cost was still far greater than that of common mortar and By intended to use Wright's cement only for pointing the lock masonry until the problem with the breastworks forced him to use it for laying new stonework and pointing and grouting the existing masonry.

To grout the masonry, all the joints were thoroughly pointed with hydraulic cement and holes were drilled horizontally into the vertical joints to take a tin tube about one-and-a-half inches in diameter. The six- to eight-foot-long tube had a right angle about eight inches from the bottom end, and a three-inch-wide flange soldered around it about two inches from the bottom end.

The tube was inserted in the hole in the masonry and clay packed around the junction. Then the tube was pushed into the hole until the flange compressed the clay into a tight seal around the tube. Grout was poured through a funnel into the top of the tube and the pressure of the head of liquid in the length of tube forced the grout into all of the cavities within the masonry. Vast quantities of hydraulic cement grout were forced into every foot of the side walls, breastwalls, masonry floors and fore and tail bays of the Rideau locks to form solid units of masonry.

Plan prop[osed for] additional Machinery for Opening the Sluices of the Lower Gates Separately; 3 September 1838

Maj. D. Bolton, R.E.
Public Archives of Canada

These gates are typical of the lower gates on the locks. As originally constructed (left gate), the sluices in the bottom of the lower gates were operated by a single rack and pinion mechanism at the top of the gate (a). It was turned by a crank handle which activated the long connecting rod (b) to open and close both pivot plate valves (c) in unison. A counterweight (d) made it easier to operate the sluices. For further ease of operation, the system was modified (right gate) in the fall of 1838; a separate mechanism was installed for each valve.

By the early 19th century, lock gates generally swung vertically about a heel post and consisted of either a single gate, on narrow locks, or a pair of gates — mitre gates — on wide locks such as those on the Rideau. Each pair of mitre gates closed at an angle pointing upstream. To ensure they met closely, the outer edges were cut on a bevel, or mitred. They were far stronger than single gates at an equivalent strength of construction and much easier to operate. Moreover, the pressure of water against their faces forced them tightly closed and thrust them back against the hollow quoin pier in which each pivoted, preventing leakage between the heel of the gate and the side wall.

Each gate was framed in heavy squared oak timbers into which heavy crossrails were mortised and reinforced with flat wrought-iron plates at the joints. The top crossrail, larger than the others, was positioned so its upper surface would be level with the water in the full lock. The face of the gate was sheeted with two-inch oak or, occasionally, pine planks.

Each gate pivoted in an iron collar strap (e) anchored to the coping of the lock wall, and on an iron pintle (f) set into a metal heel-post box in the lock floor. The pintle not only served as a pivot for the gate, but also held it several inches above the lock floor to provide the clearance required to swing it open and closed. To keep the weight of the gate from hanging on the heel-post collar, a truck, or roller wheel, (g) was bolted to the base of the bottom rail and ran on an iron track in the lock floor.

The upper gates, on the breastwork of a lock, were much shorter than the lower ones and had no sluice openings as the upper sluices were tunnels through the lock walls. Otherwise, the upper gates were the same as the lower gates, but with fewer cross rails and, occasionally, a diagonal brace.

The gates were made by either contractors' artisans, at £100 per pair of gates, or carpenters and blacksmiths on day work, under the supervision of Fitzgibbon, the master carpenter. The timber was hewn at the site and iron was supplied by the Commissariat Department, which purchased English flat iron in Montreal and heavy iron castings from the Bell foundry at Trois-Rivières. The patterns for the castings were provided by the Rideau engineering staff and the flat iron was reworked either at Bytown or, for minor work, at small forges on the locksites.

The oak in the 75 pairs of gates on the canal was of such excellent quality that the gates lasted from 15 to 22 years before the woodwork had to be renewed. Most of the present gates are close replicas of the originals, but are now constructed of Douglas fir from British Columbia.

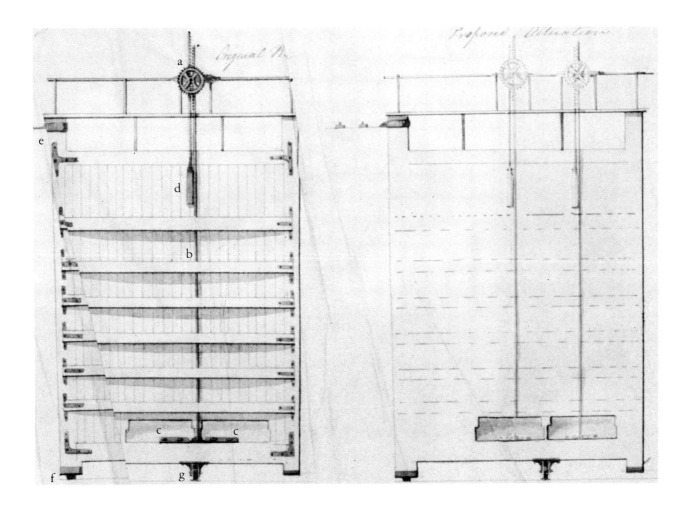

Plan and Sections of the Waste Weir acting as Dam, at First Rapids, Rideau Canal; ca. 1830

Col. John By, R.E.
Public Record Office

The timber-brace/stop-log overflow dams on the Rideau were formed by anchoring timber braces to the levelled bedrock of the river with fox bolts. The bays between the braces were closed with squared pine or hemlock stop logs laid horizontally and nailed to the front of the brace. A squared timber was anchored along the bedrock of the river against the bottom stop log. The abutments were constructed of stone masonry. To control the water level, the top two rows of stop logs were removable, as well as all the stop logs in three or four bays, permitting the water in the canal above to be lowered as required.

Contrary to the drawing, at First Rapids heavy, rough-quarried stones were piled against the back of the dam between the timber braces on either side of the bays having removable stop logs to break the fall of the water onto the riverbed. Elsewhere, heavy cut-stone masonry steps were constructed behind the stop logs for the same purpose. A clay or gravel apron was generally built up against the upstream face of the fixed stop logs.

Timber-brace overflow dams were constructed at the Hog's Back, Burritts Rapids, Merrickville, Maitland's, Smiths Falls detached lock, First Rapids and Brewers Lower Mill. All were relatively low, ranging from four to 13 feet high, and all but the Burritts Rapids dam served as combination dam/waste weirs with bays of removable stop logs. A seventh timber-brace/stop-log dam was erected at Upper Brewers Mills; however, it was exceptionally high, 18 feet, and the water did not flow over it for the water level there was regulated by a separate waste weir.

Stone arched overflow dams were constructed only at Black Rapids, Nicholsons, Clowes Quarry and Edmunds.

These relatively low dams had been undertaken early in the project before By cut costs by using timber braces and stop logs rather than arched stone masonry for the low overflow dams. Separate waste weirs were built near each of the stone arched overflow dams. In all, there were 23 waste weirs on the canal, either as part of an overflow dam or as a separate structure near an overflow or non-overflow dam. The separate weirs were built with either stone masonry or framed timber piers with grooves for the stop logs. The bays in the larger waste weirs were up to 30 feet wide.

At the time the Rideau Canal was constructed, canal engineers were undecided as to whether overflow dams maintaining a constant level of water or non-overflow dams with adjacent waste weirs were the best mode of constructing a river navigation. The Bryce Committee had expressed concern as to the exceptional height of By's proposed overflow dams, but did not question the absence of separate waste weirs.

It was known that the Rideau and Cataraqui rivers drained a large area (1500 and 200 square miles respectively) and were subject to heavy snowfalls that on the Rideau resulted in 15-foot-high spring floods, but this was not viewed as a serious objection. John Mactaggart, the clerk of works on the project, believed that the floodwaters would dissipate through the long wide stretches of river and the lakes formed by the high dams, and that the water pouring over the wide overflow dams would never be more than two feet deep.

However, By's engineering staff had not counted on the floodwater damage that threatened to undermine the dams and forced the adoption of waste weirs. The weirs

134

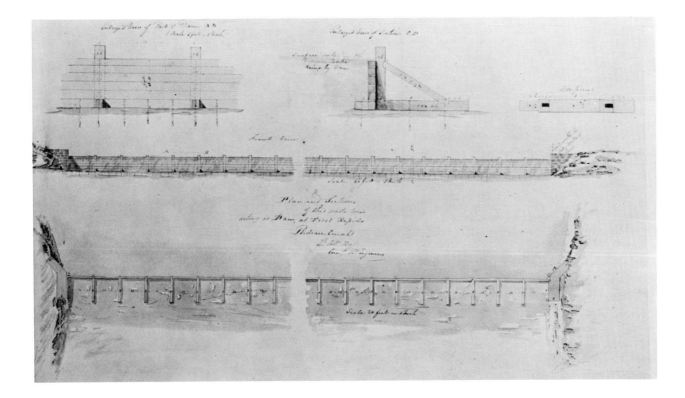

protected the dams by reducing the volume of water passing over the low overflow dams and by preventing water from flowing over the high dams.

By also initiated a flood-control system. Each fall the weirs were opened to let the water run down and were closed in the spring just before the onset of the floods. Instead of rushing unchecked down the river system, the floodwaters were absorbed in filling up the long river stretches and lake reservoirs above the dams. His system of flood control is still in use on the canal.

Plan and Elevation of Swing Bridge constructed at Merricksville over the Rideau Canal; November 1843

Lt. H. A. White, R.E.
Public Archives of Canada

The swing bridge used on the Rideau Canal in the early 1840s (see illustration) closely resembles the rolling bridges originally erected over the canal. By had planned to construct movable bridges over the locks at most of the lockstations, but this proved impossible as costs mounted. Only seven bridges were constructed as of 1832 and of these four were movable. Rolling bridges crossed lock chambers at Merrick's Mills, Maitland's and Smiths Falls, and a double-leaf drawbridge spanned the detached lock at Kingston Mills. Elsewhere on the canal were three fixed high-level bridges: the stone Sappers Bridge in Bytown, and wooden bridges at Burritts Rapids and the Isthmus. One of the first of the original rolling bridges to be replaced was that at Merrickville where the swing bridge design shown was adopted as early as 1843.

The bridge in the drawing is an unequal arm, rim-bearing swing bridge: one end of the span, the heel, is shorter than the main arm projecting across the lock chamber, and its weight is borne by the ring of roller wheels, or trucks, (a) around its turning point. The trucks ran on a ten-foot-diameter iron track fixed to a pivot pier (b) around an iron shaft (c) centered on the width of the bridge about one-third of the distance from the heel.

The bridge was swung manually by pushing on the heel. The main arm of the bridge was counterbalanced by the extra-heavy timbers in the heel and by tapering the heavy timber side stringers on the main arm to make them lighter. The span was strengthened by a king-post truss over each side stringer. Each truss consisted of an upright post, the king post (d), with chains forming the arms of the truss. The tops of the two king posts were joined by a strut. These bridges were about 65 feet long and had ten-foot-wide roadways lined with heavy railings.

The rolling bridge that the rim-bearing swing bridge replaced was of the same general configuration, but the trucks were positioned along both sides of the span and ran on two parallel iron tracks. The bridge was pulled straight back to enable the boats to pass. When closed, the toe of the rolling bridge rested on an approach ramp similar to that shown for the swing bridge and a hinged apron on its heel was swung down to meet the road. The rim-bearing swing bridges were improvements on the rolling bridges, but were still difficult to operate and in 1865 they began to be replaced by centre-bearing swing bridges.

The swing bridge was redesigned so that its weight was carried directly on an iron cone resting in an iron socket at the pivot point of the span. The ring of trucks on a circular iron track was retained, but only to stabilize the bridge; the roller wheels no longer supported its weight, making it much easier to swing. The king-post truss was retained over each of the outside stringers, which were still tapered on the main arm to reduce their weight, and the balance was improved by adding a second frame, a corbel frame, beneath the heel of the span with a heavy cross timber over the centre axis about which the bridge turned. The length of the bridge was increased to 70 feet to do away with the approach ramp projecting out from the lock wall, and the roadway was widened to 12 feet.

Today the five timber, king-post swing bridges on the canal are all replicas of the centre-bearing swing span

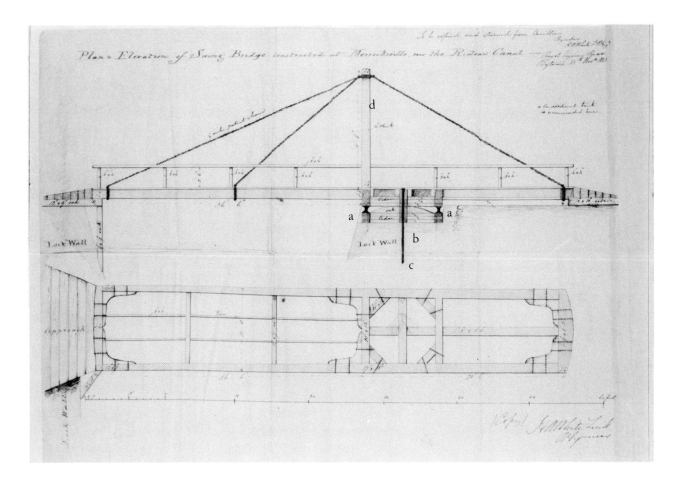

adopted in 1865. They can be seen at the Nicholsons,
Kilmarnock, Jones Falls and Lower Brewers lockstations,
and at the Brass Point crossing on Cranberry Lake.

The Great Dam at Jones' Falls; from the West end; 1841

Thomas Burrowes, watercolour, 7" × 10"
Archives of Ontario

The Jones Falls dam is the largest and finest example of the arch keywork dams constructed on the Rideau Canal. At its crest the stone arch is 62 feet high and 350 feet long between abutments. The base is 27½ feet thick, narrowing to 21½ feet at the raised water level, and it is built on a radius of 245 feet between the solid rock walls of the river gorge. The abutments were formed by excavating steps in the rock. The masonry keywork was sunk eight feet into the riverbed to secure a solid rock foundation, and was built up with blocks of dressed stone six feet by four feet by 18 inches laid on end in tightly jointed vertical courses.

The clay and earth dam raised on the upstream face of the stone arch has a 2½-to-1 slope and at its base extends some 127 feet out under the water. A clay puddle core wall about ten feet wide was planned between the earth dam and the stone arch to prevent water from penetrating the dry stone masonry; however, the core wall was eventually reduced to a thickness of five feet and the clay puddle was replaced with broken stone grouted with hydraulic cement.

The great stone arch dam at Jones Falls represents a magnificent achievement on the part of By and his engineering staff and is unique in many respects. It not only shares with the other Rideau dams of like construction the distinction of being the first arch dams in North America, Britain or France, but it was also by far the highest dam in North America at the time. Several masonry arch dams had been constructed in Spain as early as the 17th century, and one exceeded the height of the Jones Falls dam by 14 feet; however, they were constructed in relatively narrow gorges and had nowhere near the uprecedently high length-to-height ratio of the Jones Falls dam.

The Rideau arch keywork dams were also unique in being constructed, with the exception of the pointing on the Jones Falls dam, exclusively of dry stone masonry and in being composite structures. They combined the Spanish masonry arch dam with the conventional English earth dam: the upstream face of the Rideau dams consisted of the apron and puddle wall of an earth dam, but the slope of earth on the downstream side of the puddle wall was replaced by the stone arch keywork. This design probably resulted from the decision to construct the arch dams with dry stone masonry, necessitating a puddle wall to make the dam watertight, in turn necessitating an earth apron to protect the puddle.

On the Rideau Canal, nine stone arch dams were constructed, including four low overflow dams of the design initially adopted for construction, and five high dams which were raised three to six feet above the navigation level to prevent water flowing over them. With the exception of the Jones Falls dam, the high dams ranged from a height of 23 feet at Old Sly's and Smiths Falls, to 30 and 31 feet at Kingston Mills and Long Island respectively. A sixth stone arch dam of 49-foot height was undertaken at the Hog's Back, but was completed as a timber-crib dam.

Today the Jones Falls dam remains as constructed with the exception of a penstock built into one abutment for a hydro-generating plant. The other high stone arch dams survive, but only the Long Island one is clearly visible; at Old Sly's, Smiths Falls and Kingston Mills they have been almost totally obscured by land fills and embanking.

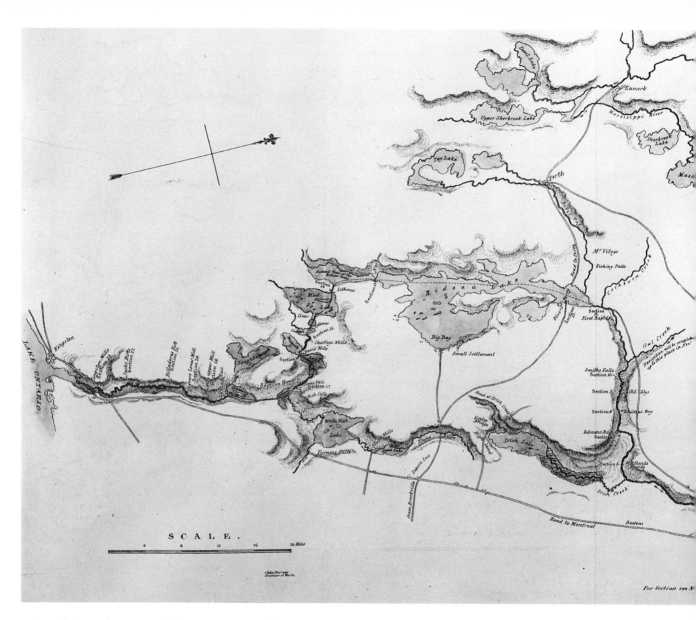

Plan of the Rideau Canal [*Cataraqui Section*]; *8 July 1830*

Col. John By, R.E.; coloured lithograph
Public Record Office

140

The Cataraqui River

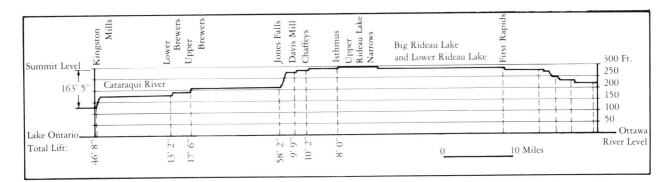

Elevation of the Rideau Canal, Cataraqui Section
S. Epps
Parks Canada

Rocky-cut at the Isthmus, to join Rideau Lake and the Waters falling into Lake Ontario; 1841

Thomas Burrowes, watercolour, 7" × 8¾"
Archives of Ontario

At the Isthmus, between Upper Rideau Lake and Mud (Newboro) Lake, a canal cut one and a half miles long connected the navigable headwaters of the Rideau and Cataraqui river systems. The excavation was 46 feet wide in rock where the banks could be vertical, and 80 feet wide in earth where the banks had to be sloped. It varied in depth from 13 to 20 feet. The painting shows the rocky banks of the cut and the piles of excavated stone at a bend near Mud Lake.

The log building on the right is an engineer's office erected during the construction period. The blockhouse in the distance is adjacent to the Isthmus lock at Mud Lake. Fixed, high- level, truss bridges of the type shown were erected at only two locksites: the Isthmus and Burritts Rapids. Just beyond the bridge, several of the earliest buildings to be erected in the village of Newboro can be seen.

The cut at the Isthmus was expected to be relatively straightforward, but it proved to be one of the most difficult works undertaken on the whole canal. Instead of earth, the Isthmus turned out to be mostly hard granite that was extremely difficult to remove. Rock was excavated by drilling holes into the rock bed and packing them with gunpowder or blasting powder. Drilling was hard, slow work, involving three-man teams turning a rock drill and driving it with a sledge hammer. Once the holes were deep enough, powder was tamped down, fuses were lit and the rock broken away by the force of the blast.

Initially men were not used to working with explosives and many serious injuries and deaths occurred. Workers were killed or maimed by flying stone, and several inexperienced men, attracted by the high wages paid for blasting work, blew themselves apart. Once the rock was blasted loose it was broken up with sledge hammers and taken out of the excavation in wheelbarrows.

The hardness of the rock escalated costs far beyond the estimate for the Isthmus canal cut. Then, to make matters worse, in the summer of 1828 malaria struck the site, bringing work to a standstill. Disease returned the next year and labourers refused to report for work.

After two contractors had abandoned the site, By placed the project under the direction of Captain Cole of the Royal Engineers. As soon as the sickly season passed, the 7th Company of Royal Sappers and Miners arrived to press on the work during the fall and winter of 1829. To aid the sappers and miners, 300 day workers were needed. By planned to attract them by constructing a hospital to care for the sick and providing good accommodations and abundant provisions. The trees were cut back 300 feet on each side of the canal to increase the circulation of fresh air.

All this, of course, entailed extra costs which were compounded when underground springs flooded the cut. Pumps had to be employed and a drainage ditch cut through solid rock. By decided to raise the Rideau Lakes summit reservoir four feet ten inches to reduce the depth of excavation at the Isthmus by building a lock at the Mud Lake end of the canal cut, and a lock and dam at the Narrows.

Residence of Cap*t*. P. Cole, R. Eng*r* the Officer in Charge at Isthmus, &c. during construction of the Works from 1830 to 1832; August 1830

T. Burrowes, watercolour, 6½" × 10⅝"
Archives of Ontario

This residence was built for Captain Cole when he took charge of the Isthmus canal cut in the fall of 1829. The house was situated on a promontory jutting out into Upper Rideau Lake. The canal cut begins a short distance in front of the land in the right foreground. The amount of land cleared to provide better air circulation can be seen in the background. Similar but much larger buildings housed the sappers and miners and day labourers working here from 1829 through 1832. The hospital was located a short distance from Cole's house.

For the first couple of years, periodic inspections of the construction sites along the Rideau were carried out from Bytown, but in June 1828 the Kempt Committee recommended that supervision of the project be more regular and more vigilant as construction began in the interior. As a result, officers of the Royal Engineers were dispersed along the waterway with each man being responsible for the daily inspection of three or four adjacent locksites.

Residences, like the one shown here, were built for the officers and full records were kept of the progress of the work. A diary was kept of the work inspected and a weekly abstract forwarded to Bytown. All checks of time and measurements of work accomplished were entered in an account book and signed by the contractor or his foreman.

A quarterly abstract was forwarded to Bytown to substantiate contractors' claims for payment. By and his clerk of works continued to make regular tours of inspection, and the master tradesmen were always des-patched to the locksites to supervise the construction and installation of breastworks, sills and gates. Any stonework found to be substandard was torn down and rebuilt properly. Only twice did work have to be placed directly under By's engineering staff — at the Hog's Back dam and the Isthmus canal cut.

Lock &c at the Isthmus, the last ascent to the Summit Water of Canal from Lake Ontario; 1841

Thomas Burrowes, watercolour, 7" × 9½"
Archives of Ontario

In the original canal layout the waters of Mud Lake were to be raised three and a half feet to the same level as the Rideau Lakes, a simple canal cut connecting the lakes. Once the decision was made to raise the summit level to save excavation work at the Isthmus, it proved impossible to raise the level of Mud Lake any further and the added height had to be obtained by placing a lock, pictured here, at the Mud Lake end of the canal cut.

By further decided to add three feet two inches to the lift of the Isthmus lock and eliminate one of the Chaffeys Mills locks downstream. The floor of the Isthmus lock was thus lowered to give it a total lift of eight feet. Both the Isthmus and the Narrows locks, at either end of the raised summit, were constructed with their upper gate sills on the same level as the lower sills so that the much larger original summit reservoir could be restored if the canal cut were ever deepened. In the absence of breastworks, the sluices were placed in the upper gates, saving the cost of tunnel sluices.

As of 1841, several minor changes had been made at the Isthmus lock. The original crab/floor-chains system of opening the gates was replaced by swing beams and a safety gate was constructed at the upper end of the lock. The safety gate, of By's own design, pivoted on a horizontal axis and lay flat on the canal bed. If the lock gates were damaged or destroyed, the surge of rushing water could cause the safety gate to swing up, blocking the canal. It could also be closed by means of the ropes and sheaves on the posts seen at either side of the lock. Several safety gates were built on the Rideau Canal.

To the right of the lock is a government storehouse, and on the opposite side a small lock office. The blockhouse was constructed in 1832-33 on the same design as the one at the Narrows. It served as a lockmaster's residence, but could house a garrison of 20 men if required. It was positioned on the knoll to enable a covering fire to be directed toward the lock to prevent marauders from destroying the lock gates and unleashing a torrent of water on the canal works farther down the system.

Other buildings erected near the blockhouse, either during the canal construction period or directly thereafter, include the cookhouse, beside the staircase, and the carpenter's building, on the left behind the pile of rock excavated from the canal cut. A root cellar, for storing vegetables during the winter, is just to the rear of the carpenter's building, and the roofs of a shed and stable are just visible on the other side of the knoll. Beyond the blockhouse, several houses can be seen in the village of Newboro, which by this time was spreading out toward Mud, renamed Newboro, Lake.

At the start of construction, there were no settlers in the Isthmus area. By 1830 over 60 log buildings were built there in keeping with By's decision to employ sappers and miners and day labourers on that difficult work. A small village sprang up near the bridge over the cut, and a number of merchants settled there, including Benjamin Tett. In 1832 Tett established a sawmill and a store complex at Buttermilk Falls (Bedford Mills) at the opposite end of Newboro Lake, and became involved in the forwarding business on the Rideau Canal. By 1850

Newboro had a population of 300 persons whose livelihood depended on the transport facilities provided by the canal for grain, squared timber, and lumber.

Today only the blockhouse and lock chamber remain of the Isthmus canal structures. The blockhouse was taken down to its masonry walls in 1967 and the upper storey re-built with B.C. fir. The outside staircase was reconstructed and a door cut through one of the masonry walls. In 1966-67, the manually operated wooden lock gates were replaced by hydraulically operated steel gates, and a modern lock office was constructed on the site.

Chaffey's Mills August 1827

[Thomas Burrowes], pencil sketch, 6½" × 9½"
Baird Papers, Archives of Ontario

From the Isthmus the canal was routed through Mud (Newboro) Lake into Clear Lake where a second canal cut, 180 feet long by six feet deep, was made through earth to provide a direct entrance into Indian Lake. The three interconnected lakes were all on the same level and just over five feet deep, with low rocky banks interspersed with swamps and marshlands. They flowed into a fourth small lake, Mosquito (Opinicon) Lake, through a boulder-strewn channel where the river dropped 13 feet in 333 yards. Here, four and a half miles from the Isthmus and 44 miles from Kingston, Samuel Chaffey had established a mill complex. The milldam, built across the river just upstream of the bridge, established the water level for the lakes between Chaffeys Mills and the Isthmus.

Samuel Chaffey came from a family of woolen manufacturers in Somerset, England, several members of which emigrated to Upper Canada at the close of the War of 1812. In 1827 his mill complex consisted of a grist and carding mill on one bank of the river and a sawmill and distillery on the opposite bank. Four dwellings and a barn adjacent to the mills provided the basis of a small self-sufficient settlement. Chaffeys Mills was totally isolated during the summer, but in winter farmers brought their grain by sleigh on paths cut through the forest. In the absence of an efficient road or water transport system, the flour ground at the mills was consumed locally.

Initially By planned the layout of dams and locks so that Chaffey's mill complex would be undisturbed. A stone arch overflow dam was to be constructed above the complex, with a lock in a canal cut passing around the mills and back into the river where a second overflow dam and lock were required to flood the base of the rapids below the milldam.

However, in 1827 the miller died of malaria and his widow sold the buildings and 200 adjacent acres to By for a reasonable price. This enabled By to remove the mill complex and simplify the canal layout to effect major savings. In conjunction with the decision to add over three feet to the Isthmus lock's lift, and the discovery of an error in levels, it proved possible to build a single lock of 11-foot lift just below the former mill site, along with a single ten-foot-high dam and a waste weir. Of the structures shown in the drawing, only the four dwellings escaped demolition in 1829.

Chaffey's Mills

149

Lock, Waste-weir &c at Chaffey's Mills; Sketched 1833, Col[oured] Jan[y]. 1841

Thomas Burrowes, watercolour, 6½" × 9½"
Archives of Ontario

Chaffeys Mills was one of the unhealthiest construction sites on the entire waterway. The works were contracted to John Haggart, a stonemason and miller from Perth, and his partner John Sheriff. At first construction proceeded rapidly but in August 1828, malaria broke out, claiming the lives of Sheriff and several labourers.

Malaria, sometimes called swamp fever or ague, was the worst affliction suffered by men working on the Rideau project. It occurred every year about mid-August and lasted until mid-September. Once caught, it lasted for months with the sufferer totally incapacitated during that time and subject to relapses. The overall mortality rate was comparatively low on the project as a whole, about four per cent a year, but at some of the Cataraqui sites no one escaped the fever's ill-effects and the death rate soared.

The symptoms were graphically described by John Mactaggart:

The Fever and Ague of Canada are different, I am told, from those of other countries; they generally come on with an attack of bilious fever, dreadful vomiting, pains in the back and loins, general debility, loss of appetite, so that one cannot even take tea . . . . After being in this state for eight or ten days, the yellow jaundice is likely to ensue, then fits of trembling . . . . For two or three hours before they arrive, we feel so cold that nothing will warm us; the greatest heat that be applied is perfectly unfelt . . . . Our very bones ache, teeth chatter, and the ribs are sore, continuing thus in great agony for about an hour and a half; we then commonly have to vomit, the trembling ends, and a profuse sweat ensues, which lasts for two hours longer. This over, we find the malady has run one of its rounds, and start out of the bed in a feeble state.

Malaria was not confined to the Rideau; it was found in swampy areas across Upper Canada. In the hot summer of 1828 its impact was severe from York (Toronto) to Kingston, and in Perth it was reported that every house was like a hospital. Malaria continued to infect southern and eastern Upper Canada until well into the 1870s, when the disappearance of swamp lands and better sanitation succeeded in eradicating it.

Construction moved ahead on the Chaffeys Mills site despite the malaria and a lock of ten-foot two-inch lift was finally finished. The painting shows the lock, as well as a waste channel and weir cut in the riverbank to control water levels above the lock. The 33-foot-wide steamboat lock with its wing walls extended was sufficiently wide to block the river, eliminating the need for a dam. The flow of water through the weir was regulated with stop logs which rested in grooves built into the face of the masonry abutments.

Many Rideau weirs were similarly constructed, although some had multiple stop-log bays. Initially the squared stop logs were manhandled into position, but later a crab with hook and chain was installed on each abutment to manipulate them. The log buildings along the edge of the river housed canal workers and were located just in front of the dwellings built earlier by Chaffey.

150

Opinicon Lake, looking to N:W:; November 1840

Thomas Burrowes, watercolour, 6¾" × 9¾"
Archives of Ontario

The *Hunter,* seen crossing Opinicon Lake on its way to Bytown, is typical of the multi-purpose steamers serving the canal. The early Rideau steamboats closely approximated the Ottawa River steamboats: 108-foot-long, 30-foot-wide sidewheelers. They had up to 25-horsepower engines, could travel five miles an hour, and could tow three or four fully laden Durham boats. Each steamboat was capable of carrying over 90 barrels of cargo or 70 to 80 passengers. The *Hunter,* built at Prescott in 1838, had passenger cabins, an upper promenade deck and a freight hold.

When the Rideau Canal opened in May 1832, there were only two small steamboats on the canal, the *Union* and the *Pumper.* In August Robert Drummond, the former Kingston Mills contractor, began operating the *Rideau* and in 1833 launched the *Margaret* to initiate a bi-weekly service between Kingston and Bytown. Subsequently, the *Enterprise* of Perth and the *Thomas McKay* plied the canal.

When Drummond died in the cholera epidemic of August 1834, his two vessels were purchased by the Ottawa Steamboat Company, which in 1835 became The Ottawa and Rideau Forwarding Company (ORF) and boasted four steamboats in regular service on the Rideau Canal (the *Thomas McKay, Rideau, Margaret* and *Bytown*) and three on the Ottawa River (the *Shannon, Ottawa* and *St. Andrews*) engaged in a triangular trade whereby Durham boats and barges were loaded with merchandise and immigrants at Montreal and towed up the Ottawa-Rideau system to Kingston where they were laden with produce and sent back down the St. Lawrence to Montreal.

The ORF was operated by a group of prominent Montrealers, among whom were John Redpath (the Jones Falls contractor), John Molson (the builder of the first steamboat in British North America), and Thomas Phillips (probably the Black Rapids/Long Island contractor). Initially the company enjoyed a monopoly of steam towing on the Ottawa-Rideau system, but Rideau Canal traffic continued to grow despite the political troubles and depressed economy of 1836-37 and by 1841 six forwarding companies were busy on the Montreal-Bytown-Kingston triangle. These included the ORF, in partnership with an old established St. Lawrence forwarding company, Mac-Pherson and Crane, as well as Hooker and Henderson of Kingston, J. Jones and Company of Brockville, Sanderson and Murray, William Dickinson and Company, and McGibbon and Ferguson, operating a total of 19 steamers, 171 tow barges, and three self-propelled barges.

Although it generally took four to five days for freight barges to be towed from Montreal to Kingston, steamers running day and night could complete the Rideau section of the trip in 34½ hours. A typical Rideau run was that of the steamboat *Perth.* It left Kingston on Tuesdays at 9 a.m., calling at Kingston Mills, Upper Brewers, Jones Falls, the Isthmus, Oliver's Ferry, Port Elmsley, Smiths Falls, Merrickville, Burritts Rapids, Becket's Landing, and Long Island, and arriving in Bytown on Wednesdays at 7:30 p.m.

On the return trip, it left Bytown at 9 a.m. Fridays, stopping at the same places enroute, and arriving at Kingston the next day at 8:30 p.m. In 1848 the time was cut still further when Hooker and Henderson launched the *Prince Albert,* a fast passenger steamer which ran on a 27-hour schedule between Bytown and Kingston, completing two round trips per week.

The proliferation of steamboats and barges was not without its drawbacks. In a 24-hour period, as many as five

steamers, each towing from four to eight barges, could arrive at one locksite, forcing the lock labourers at a major site, such as Jones Falls, to work up to 15 hours during the course of a day. With the canal operating 24 hours a day, seven days a week, the labourers had no regular hours of rest so in 1844 the Ordnance closed the canal from 10 p.m. to 6 a.m. each day. However, the forwarders raised such an outcry that the around-the-clock schedule was reinstated.

Over the years the Rideau steamboats underwent numerous changes. By the 1840s the side paddlewheels began to give way to screw propellers, and by the 1850s the multi-purpose steamers were replaced by steamers designed for specific functions: tugs, freight boats and passenger vessels.

In the 1890s the first of the luxury excursion steamers, the *James Swift*, was launched. Renamed the *Rideau King* in 1901, it and its sister ships, such as the *Rideau Queen*, *John Haggart* and the *Ottawan*, had panelled berths, lounges and dining rooms, and carried up to 350 passengers on three-day cruises along the canal. The last of these, the *Ottawan*, was retired in 1936, bringing to a close over 100 years of steamboat operation on the Rideau Canal.

Davis' Mill, Lock &c: looking towards Kingston; Sketched Novr 1840, Co[loured] Dec^r /40

Thomas Burrowes, watercolour, 6½" × 11¼"
Archives of Ontario

Prior to the construction of the canal, the river between Opinicon and Sand lakes fell seven and a half feet through a rocky glen. The rapids were discovered by Americans searching for timber and here one of them, Walter Davis, settled in 1800. Davis, the only settler in the immediate area, built a house on the rocky knoll, a sawmill on the riverbank at its base, and a milldam across the river just above the mill.

When By laid out the canal he hoped to avoid disturbing the sawmill but once again disease and excavation difficulties inflated costs. Most of the 45-man work force was incapacitated by malaria each fall and, as at Chaffeys Mills, all of the excavation work was in hard limestone mixed with granite. With costs exceeding the contract prices, the contractor withdrew and the Davis Mills contract was let again in 1830 to a new partnership of John Haggart and Robert Drummond.

To speed construction and save money, By purchased and demolished the mill. A proposed arched dam was replaced by two simple dry-stone walls with clay puddle packed between them, and a canal cut was abandoned in favour of positioning a single lock and dam on the former mill site. A waste weir channel was cut around a knoll at the opposite end of the dam which, in conjunction with the lock of nine-foot nine-inch lift, created a navigable body of water across Opinicon Lake to Chaffeys Mills.

In the painting the canal structures are shown with Sand Lake in the background. By 1840 a storehouse had been erected to the right of the lock, and a lockmaster's house, which may have been erected as the contractor's residence, on the knoll at the opposite end of the dam. To its rear is a stable with a lean-to extension on the bank of the waste water channel, passing around the knoll and into the river below the dam.

The waste weir has multiple stop-log bays to control the water level and a bridge to provide access to the locksite. To the front of the weir is a log boom that prevented floating logs and debris from clogging the weir. The building on the far side of the weir is probably a barn. On both banks of the canal the land cleared to provide better air circulation during the canal construction period contrasts with the heavy forest below the locksite.

Today the Davis locksite remains relatively isolated, only a dirt road and the canal providing access. The layout of the canal has not been altered, but the structures have been. All of the buildings shown in the 1840 drawing have been demolished, beginning with the lockmaster's house which was replaced during the 1840s with a defensible lockmaster's house. The storehouse, to the right of the lock, was replaced circa 1900 by the existing one-and-a-half storey frame storehouse situated at the opposite end of the dam.

During the 19th century, dredging debris was dumped behind the dam; now covered in grass, it appears to be a natural embankment rather than a man-made structure. The wood-plank flooring of the lock was replaced with a concrete cap near the turn of the century, and after a succession of wood-frame waste weirs, the present concrete weir was constructed in the 1930s.

Lock, &c at Davis's Mill; Repairing the Gates & Wooden bottom of Lock; winter of 1843-4

Thomas Burrowes, watercolour, 7" × 9¾"
Archives of Ontario

In this winter scene a work crew is maintaining the lock at Davis Mill. At the edge of the lockpit men are squaring and mortising a timber which will be used to construct new lock gates. A horse and ox team is drawing more rough-hewn timbers from the local forest to the site and, below the lock, men are removing debris preparatory to renewing the wooden lock floor. The lock remains as constructed with the exception of the curved-swing-bar/ crab system of operating the lock gates, and the water has been lowered in keeping with By's flood control system.

During the 19th century the Rideau Canal was widely acclaimed as one of the finest canals ever built and its maintenance record bears that out. A decade after its construction, it cost only £9270 per year to maintain and operate, exclusive of flood damages. In contrast, over £94,500 was spent repairing the Welland Canal during its first four years of operation.

Only a few relatively minor structural failures have occurred on the Rideau Canal over the years. Exceptionally severe flooding took place from time to time and on each occasion driftwood and ice floes borne on the crest of the flood broke through protecting booms and breached several waste weirs. None of the high stone arch dams were ever damaged, however, and only one waste weir, the Long Island weir, suffered repeated injury. The other weirs and the low overflow dams suffered only random, readily repairable damage and many of the stone weirs and overflow dams were not replaced until well into the 20th century. Most of the 47 locks have continued to function to the present day with but minor repairs or partial rebuilding and renewal of the stonework.

The canal is a credit to By's capabilities as an engineer and a measure of his capacity to organize and supervise, together with his overseers and fellow officers of the Royal Engineers, a work of the magnitude of the Rideau Canal where for the better part of six years uniformly high standards of construction were enforced and direction given to more than 4500 men scattered over two dozen worksites along a waterway winding through 123 miles of wilderness and swamps.

His achievement is all the more amazing when it is considered that five of the initial 18 major contractors abandoned their contracts and two died of malaria. Only four of the 18 completed their contracts satisfactorily, and the contribution of these men — Thomas McKay, John Redpath, the partnership of Thomas Phillips and Andrew White, and Robert Drummond — was publicly recognized when By presented silver cups to them at the conclusion of the project.

Jones Falls; post-1843

William Clegg, watercolour, 8¾" × 12¼"
Public Archives of Canada, C-1219

At Jones Falls, four miles from Davis Mills, the waters of Sand Lake dropped 60 feet into Cranberry Marsh through a long, rocky gorge with steep banks up to 90 feet high. Jones Falls was named after an absentee landowner, and when By first viewed the site in May 1827, it was in the centre of a wilderness. Reuben Sherwood, the surveyor who guided By on his first tour of the proposed canal route, was given a preliminary contract to clear the site, open access roads and search for stone suitable for quarrying. The main contract was awarded to John Redpath, an experienced masonry contractor.

By considered the works at Jones Falls to be the boldest and most daring on the whole Rideau system. His original plans for the site were disrupted by the Kempt Committee's decision to enlarge the locks on the waterway. This left insufficient space for the six locks, each of ten-foot lift, that By proposed and so he had to adopt a new layout. As the painting shows, three locks, one of 13 and two of 15-foot lift, carried the canal to a natural basin and a fourth, of 15-foot, two-inch lift, raised it to the level of the water backed up by the dam. At the time, a 15-foot lift was considered dangerously high and stronger gates were made for each lock.

The high rocky banks at Jones Falls consisted mostly of sandstone and granite, but the locks and waste weirs had to be carried through a hard granite that almost doubled excavation costs. Moreover, the nearest sandstone suitable for quarrying was six miles distant. By had no choice but to increase the contract price for the rock excavation and to assume the costs for moving the stone from the quarry to the locksite. The price paid for clay puddle also had to be increased to cover transport costs as the huge amounts required for the core wall of the dam rapidly used up the clay deposits found nearby.

Each fall, these construction problems were exacerbated with the onset of the malaria that struck Jones Falls as severely as the other Cataraqui locksites. During the 1828 sickly season, the whole work force was incapacitated, and in succeeding years up to three-quarters of the 260 men on the site were too ill to work.

To the left of the upper lock in the painting is a small storehouse and a blacksmith's shop erected in 1843 to enable rapid repairs to be made to any damaged lock gates. The defensible lockmaster's house on the opposite side of the lock was built in 1841. On the rocky knoll beside the basin is the guardhouse. On the opposite side of the dam, above the main river channel, are two lock labourers' houses, a stable and several ruins. These buildings were constructed to house the contractor and his foremen. The accommodations for the workmen were on the lock basin near the blacksmith's shop, and may well have been demolished when that structure was built.

Neither of the two waste weirs is shown. The upper waste channel was cut from above the upper lock, through the rock to the rear of the lockmaster's house, and into the river channel below the dam. The lower waste channel passes from the basin, behind the guardhouse, to the river.

Today the Jones Falls locks and the 62-foot-high stone arch dam remain virtually as constructed. The original storehouse and guardhouse have been demolished, but the blacksmith's shop and defensible lockmaster's house survive and have been restored. The waste weirs have been renewed in concrete. A timber swing bridge can be found adjacent to the middle combined lock. The swing

bridge and the road bridge across the canal beside the
bottom lock are replicas of the original bridges erected in
1883 to connect the locksite with the Hotel Kenney
established in 1878.

The Drowned Land — Rideau Canal 4 August 1844

Major George Seton, 93rd Regiment of Foot; watercolour, 6¼" × 9¼"
Public Archives of Canada, C-1073

Below Jones Falls, the Rideau Canal passed through an oblong marsh eight miles long by two miles wide, narrowing at its mid-point. The upper part of the marsh, the Drowned Lands, consisted of dead standing trees, floating islands of moss and reeds, and tangles of dead tree limbs that gave the site a desolate appearance relieved only by herons nesting in the tree tops. In the illustration the Drowned Lands are depicted after the water level was raised two feet and a wide channel cleared for the passage of steamboats. In the background is the steamboat *Pumper*.

The lower half of the marsh, Cranberry Marsh, was covered in floating masses of cranberry bushes with long tangled roots that made it difficult for even canoes to force a passage. The waters that inundated the marshland were backed up by timber dams that lumbermen had erected at its two outlets: the Round Tail, at the lower end of Cranberry Marsh where the Cataraqui River began, and White Fish Falls, on the Drowned Lands section where the Gananoque River began.

It initially appeared that carrying the canal through the Drowned Lands and Cranberry Marsh would require only cutting the dead trees and cranberry bushes to form a clear channel, removing the Round Tail dam, and reconstructing the White Fish Falls dam in a more substantial manner. The water level in the marsh was to be maintained by the new White Fish Falls weir and by canal structures on the Cataraqui River at Upper Brewers Mills, one mile below the Round Tail. The contract was let in February 1828 to John Brewer, the mill proprietor.

Brewer removed the dams and commenced clearing the canal channel; however, the work proved much more difficult than anticipated. In Cranberry Marsh the men had to work in a heavy noxious mist and wade through a blue slime that when disturbed gave off odour that Mactaggart likened to "a cadaverous animal in the last stages of decomposition." The men had to work and live in such an environment, which unfortunately proved all too typical of what was found in excavations in the marshlands and swamps formed by the milldams along the Cataraqui. To the dysentery prevalent at such sites was added the scourge of blackflies in the late spring and the swarms of mosquitoes in the warm weather, but even these torments paled when measured against the terrible impact of malaria that struck each August.

During the exceptionally hot summer of 1828, malaria brought work to a complete standstill on the Cataraqui. The entire work force fell ill and a number of men died.

It is not known precisely how many died of malaria in 1828 or over the course of the project as By refused to gather such statistics for fear of scaring off new workers who were needed to replace the dead. Partial statistics gathered in 1830 for the Cataraqui locksites indicated that with the onset of the sickly season each year, anywhere from a tenth to a half of the work force departed. Most of these were probably local settlers and French Canadians who could return to their homes; the Irish and other immigrants, totally dependent on wage labour for their subsistence, remained on the job.

At the Isthmus canal cut, 601 men worked during the 1830 sickly season and 27 died, as well as 13 women and 15 children. Elsewhere the number of deaths varied widely from 30 out of a workforce of 80 men at Jack's Rifts, to 12 out of 100 men at Kingston Mills. The partial returns indicate that as many as 500 men, exclusive of women and children who were present at several of the locksites, may

have died of malaria over the course of the project.

No one on the Cataraqui escaped malaria. The engineering department, the contractors, the overseers and the labourers were all incapacitated. In September 1829 even By's life was despaired of when he suffered a severe bout that left his health permanently impaired. The malaria not only delayed completion of the project, but also killed a number of highly skilled artificers who were difficult to replace. The deaths of several contractors and the failure of others, discouraged by the sickness and extremely difficult rock work, forced By to add up to 600 labourers to his establishment to carry on.

Higher costs were also incurred after 1830 in pursuing winter excavation work to avoid the sickly season, paying higher prices to induce new contractors to take over the unhealthy worksites, paying higher wages, and providing medical attention and as many comforts as possible to encourage workers to stay on the job. All of these factors combined to produce cost overruns on the project, but none were relatively so large as at the Cranberry Marsh where work estimated at £1409 in 1828 eventually cost £77,342 to complete.

Wooden Dam at the White Fish Falls; — and Blockhouse [Guardhouse] to protect it; 1839

Thomas Burrowes, watercolour, 6¼" × 9¼"
Archives of Ontario

At the White Fish Falls, where the Gananoque River flowed out of the Drowned Lands, By built a timber frame waste weir to raise the water level of the marsh and obtain a navigable depth from Jones Falls to Upper Brewers Mills on the Cataraqui. By intended the weir to be the major regulating weir on the system through which the flood-waters passing down the Cataraqui could be diverted into the Gananoque River system. It was built on the site of an earlier milldam and appears to have had a timber slide at one end.

In the aftermath of the 1837 rebellions, the military acted quickly to garrison the four blockhouses By erected on the canal and provide defences for the critical works at White Fish Falls and Jones Falls. In July 1838, militia forces were called out and guardhouses were built at both sites to accommodate them. The White Fish Falls guard-house was occupied by a succession of militia units, comprising a sergeant and anywhere from eight to 13 men from 1838 to 1843, after which a one-man guard was stationed there until 1856 when the Ordnance turned the canal over to the province. Thereafter, the guardhouse was rented out, fell into disrepair, and was eventually de-molished.

In the early 19th century it was believed that malaria was caused by noxious swamp air. Indeed, the very word was derived from the Italian *mala aria,* meaning "bad air." Hence when malaria struck, By's first effort to protect the workers consisted of cutting back the trees at the work sites to improve the air circulation. Swamps were drained to eliminate the mists and the height of the works at most Cataraqui locksites was substantially increased to flood intervening swamps and eliminate the need for extensive excavations there.

Such efforts ultimately did help eradicate malaria by eliminating mosquito-breeding areas, but more immediate measures had to be taken to aid stricken workers. The Ordnance withheld a small fraction of the wages paid to artificers and labourers employed directly by the Royal Engineer establishment to provide for medical attention, medicines and hospitalization for the men and subsistence for their families in the event they were incapacitated through illness or accident.

No provision had been made for contractor's workers or for casual labourers hired by the department, but once malaria struck, By ordered the medical officer to tend all the sick, regardless of whether or not they were covered by the Ordnance regulation, and to admit them to the hospital at Bytown where they were to be put on the charge of the military chest if not covered by stoppages.

A second hospital, at the Isthmus, was built and monies due the contractors were held back to pay for medical supplies and hospitalization for their sick and injured workers. Ailing casual workers were carried on the Rideau accounts. For the most part, hospitalization amounted to simply feeding and providing the most basic care for the patients to prevent them from dying of neglect and exposure, if not starvation. Little more could be done as quinine was too expensive: it sold for $16 an ounce.

Brewer's Upper Mills: Upper Lock partly built, Excavations, Embankments &c in progress; May 1830

Thomas Burrowes, watercolour, 6½" × 9½"
Archives of Ontario

A mile below Cranberry Marsh on the Cataraqui River the water fell almost ten feet through a stretch of rapids. In 1802 John Brewer settled at this spot and by 1826 had a sawmill, brewery and grist mill in operation supporting a small settlement. Most of the buildings in the painting predate the canal and those on the upper course of the river are probably Brewer's. The circular stone structure is a lime kiln, such as were constructed at various locksites to make mortar from limestone. The other buildings are either dwellings, barns, stables or storage buildings.

The works at Upper Brewers Mills backed up the river at a navigable depth through Cranberry Marsh and the Drowned Lands to Jones Falls, a distance of 11 miles. By initially planned to avoid the mill complex, but Brewer was awarded the contract for construction at the site and he afterwards agreed to sell his mill and lands. This allowed By to construct an 18-foot-high dam across the river at the site of the former milldam.

A cut on the right bank carried the canal around the rapids and two locks raised the level 17½ feet. The canal excavation can be seen on the left in the painting. The lockpits were excavated in clay with pick and shovel, and the clay removed in wheelbarrows, making use of wheeling planks. The excavated material, including rock from further up the cut, was dumped on either side of the excavation to form embankments.

The major embankment, nine feet high by 176 yards long, had to be built up along the river side of the canal, and was carried in a semicircle just above the locks to form a basin. An impermeable clay puddle core wall, several feet thick, was constructed in each embankment. At the time the drawing was done, the timber sleepers of the upper lock floor had been laid on macadamized stone and the wall masonry raised several feet. The lower lockpit was still being excavated.

Construction proceeded slowly as Brewer proved a meticulous craftsman and malaria was rife. In most years, anywhere from one-half to all of the 113-man work force was unable to work during the sickly season, and Brewer began to experience financial difficulties which in 1831 caused him to flee the country. His departure forced By to increase the contract price for masonry work before Robert Drummond, the Kingston Mills contractor, would agree to take over the job. The works were not completed until the spring of 1832.

Like Chaffeys Mills, Upper Brewers Mills was a settlement that was actually harmed by the construction of the canal. With the mills rendered inoperable, the site was soon abandoned.

Settlement revived at mid-century when William Anglin of Kingston erected a major sawmill complex, but the depletion of the forest reserves forced its closure by the 1890s. Today no evidence remains of the industrial complexes, but the former military importance of the canal is still evident at the upper end of the canal cut where a defensible lockmaster's house was erected in 1842. Otherwise, only the canal structures, a hydro-generating plant built in 1939, and a modern lock office intrude on a pastoral setting. The dam, replaced during the 19th century, is covered with grass and shrubs, as is the embankment, and both appear to be part of the natural landscape. The basin and locks remain as constructed, but

the wooden floors of the locks have been capped in
concrete.

Brewer's Lower Mill: Masonry of the Lock nearly completed, Excavation for Canal in progress, 1831-2

Thomas Burrowes, watercolour, 6¼" × 9½"
Archives of Ontario

From Upper Brewers Mills to Kingston Mills the Cataraqui was rather narrow, about 60 feet wide, and wound between low clay banks and across several large swamps and low lands of standing dead timber. Except in the dry summer months, the river was a navigable depth and it appeared that all that would be required was some minor excavation along the river, and the erection of canal structures at Lower Brewers, Kingston Mills and, between these sites, at two rough-water shallows: Billidore's Rift, four miles below Lower Brewers, and Jack's Rift, several miles further downstream.

Prior to the construction of the Rideau Canal, there was a sawmill, dam and two dwellings at Lower Brewers Mill, two and three-quarter miles below Brewers upper mill complex. By once again planned to bypass the mill but eventually bought it so that canal structures could be located to take better advantage of the terrain.

The original contractor at the site was Samuel Clowes. He set to work with a force of 80 men; however, the excavation in the riverbed gave off a nauseous odour and during the first summer many labourers were stricken with malaria. Clowes himself died of the disease and his contract was taken over by Robert Drummond of Kingston Mills who completed the works: a wood-frame waste weir of 13-foot height, a wood-floored lock of 13-foot 2-inch lift and an extensive line of embankments from five to nine feet high. The several buildings in the flood area above the lock and waste weir were demolished and the sawmill was left a standing ruin.

The watercolour shows the sawmill still standing on the riverbank in the background. The canal cut, with the lock at its lower end, crossed a sharp bend in the river, carrying the canal past the rapids below the milldam. The excavation for the cut has barely begun, but the lock masonry is almost complete. The curved wing walls at either end of the lock and the side wall details are clearly visible. The coffer dam across the lower end of the lock is still in place, and the sheer poles, block and tackle, ropes and crabs used to manoeuvre the heavy stone blocks have yet to be removed. Below the lock, labourers are cutting across a small bend in the river to provide a direct entrance into the lock chamber.

The log buildings housed the canal workers and the whitewashed house between the lock and sawmill was probably the contractor's residence. Soon after this sketch was made, the waste weir was constructed on the milldam site, and embankments were extended from the high land near the tree line to the weir, between the weir and the lock, and from the lock to the high land in the right foreground.

The lockmaster, lock labourers, and their families were the sole occupants of the Lower Brewers (later renamed Washburn) locksite until 1861 when James Foster erected a grist mill and, later, a woollen mill and store there. The grist mill is still standing today, beside a hydro-electric powerhouse that utilized the surplus waste-weir water from 1942 to 1970.

The only other buildings on the site are a defensible lockmaster's house, erected in the late 1840s, and a clapboarded house built circa 1930. A second storey and several additions were made to the lockmaster's house in the late 19th century. A poor foundation under the Lower

Brewers lock necessitated frequent repairs over the years, culminating in a complete reconstruction in 1977 using stone from the original structure.

Kingston Mills: Masonry of three lower locks completed, Steamboat "Pumper" at lock entrance; ca. 1830

Thomas Burrowes, watercolour, 5" × 9¼"
Archives of Ontario

At Kingston Mills the Cataraqui wound through a low-lying marshland and fell 17 feet over a granite ledge into a deep rocky gorge at the head of an inlet stretching four and a half miles inland from Lake Ontario. In 1783-84 the British Government had erected a sawmill and grist mill at the site to serve the Loyalist settlement and naval dockyard being founded at Kingston. Kingston Mills, the last locksite on the descent from Upper Rideau Lake to Lake Ontario, became one of the major sites on the canal.

By had planned to construct an 11-foot-high dam above the falls with three locks in a canal cut carrying the navigation down 28 feet to the level of Lake Ontario. However, the extreme hardness of the granite rock and the devastating impact of malaria in the excavations upstream forced him to raise the water level substantially to flood the river, eliminating the canal works at Jack's and Billidore's rifts and reducing the rock excavation at Kingston Mills. Thus, three combined locks, a detached lock, a 30-foot-high stone arch dam and two extensive embankments were constructed to raise the canal 46 feet 8 inches above Lake Ontario and back up a navigable depth of water the ten miles to Lower Brewers Mill.

In the drawing, the three combined locks have been constructed parallel to the head of the inlet. The coffer dam is still in place at the entrance to the bottom lock where the steamboat *Pumper* is running its pumps to keep the lock chamber dry. Above the combined locks a curved embankment is being raised to form an intermediate basin to connect them with the detached lock on which excavation work has just begun. The two squat circular structures beside the basin embankment are probably lime kilns. An embankment remains to be constructed to prevent the raised water flowing across the low-lying land to the left of the detached lock.

To the right of the detached lock, the dam is under construction across the original river channel, on the far side of which a long embankment has already been erected to prevent the raised waters from flowing around the end of the dam. A masonry waste weir remains to be constructed at the junction of the dam and embankment.

To the right of the gap between the dam and embankment is the original mill dwelling, and just below where the river fell into the inlet is the sawmill with a timber slide barely visible nearby. The grist mill was destroyed by fire at an earlier date. The canal buildings were erected on the far left of the site and include workshops, bunkhouses, the office of Lieutenant Briscoe, who supervised the site, a schoolhouse, and the home of Robert Drummond, the contractor, and his family.

The sawmill was not damaged during construction and when it resumed operation once the waters were raised in the canal, a small village grew up at Kingston Mills. Two taverns and a dozen houses were scattered along the Kingston-Montreal road, which crossed the canal at the locksite. In 1853 the Grand Trunk Railway erected a bridge over the combined locks and in the late 19th century a grist mill was built near the sawmill.

Otherwise, with the exception of the replacement of several of the canal buildings, the locksite remained unchanged until 1913 when a powerhouse was constructed below the waste weir, the grist mill was demolished, and a new dam and weir constructed to the rear of the canal

structures, totally transforming the landscape. The original drawbridge over the detached lock has been replaced by a series of swing bridges. A blockhouse, erected beside the detached lock in 1832, still stands and has been restored to its original appearance.

Rideau Canal [Kingston Mills]; sketched fall of 1831

Lt. E. C. Frome, R.E.; watercolour, 6¼" × 9¾"
The Royal Commonwealth Society

Frome drew the Kingston Mills locksite after the water was raised in the canal. The three combined locks, upper detached lock, and canal basin with a dry-dock extension, have been completed as have the stone arch dam and masonry waste weir, at the far right, to carry surplus water down the original watercourse.

On the far left is the lockmaster's house, formerly Drummond's house, which was connected by a fixed bridge (not visible) across the raised waters to the workshop on the Kingston-Montreal road. At the head of the dry dock is an office built in 1831 when Kingston Mills became the operations headquarters for the Cataraqui section of the canal. A blockhouse erected to the right of the detached lock in 1832 is not shown as it postdates the pencil sketch on which the watercolour is based.

The watercolour faithfully reproduces the detail of the sketch with the exception of the figures added to provide perspective and the water leaking through the lock gates. The rustic leaky gates are a touch of the picturesque more in keeping with the work of contemporary Romantic movement watercolourists than the precise, purposive paintings associated with military artists and topographers.

The only significant inaccuracy is the depiction of the long timber bridge above the basin. An earth embankment topped by a post-and-rail fence had been raised to the left of the upper lock and the actual timber bridge ran, level with the lock coping, from the drawbridge over the upper lock across the river below the dam. Frome's confusion resulted from the incomplete state of his sketch, and his lack of familiarity with the site owing to his having served on the Rideau section of the canal during the construction period. With the exception of the picturesque element and the inaccurate bridge, his watercolour is typical of the work the Royal Engineers were trained to produce.

Officer cadets at the Royal Military Academy were required to become proficient in draughting and topographical drawing. In a pre-camera age, it was essential that officers be able to produce field sketches that accurately depicted the features — ridges, roads, watercourses, contours, vegetation and structures — of a potential battlefield clearly and comprehensively. Generally, this took the form of rapid pencil or pen and ink sketches made on the spot and coloured directly thereafter to make the features more recognizable.

Watercolours were used because they were easy to carry and the materials required — the colours, water and a binding element, usually lime — could be obtained almost anywhere. At Woolwich the cadets studied under Paul Sandby (1730-1809), "the father of English watercolourists," who set exceptionally high standards for his cadets and succeeding drawing masters. Sandby's courses included "Indian Ink landscapes, Large coloured landscapes, Naturally coloured landscapes, Perspective in drawing buildings and fortifications, Embellishment of landscapes for military purposes, and the Practice and Theory of Perspective." Figures were not taught, which no doubt accounts for their general absence, and the stick-like appearance of the few shown, in the Rideau watercolours.

Sandby taught three basic watercolour techniques: grey wash, body-colour and aquatint. In the first process, a sketch was made in pencil or chalk point and shadows were added with a grey wash before the colours were applied, giving the work a luminous effect. In the body-colour process, the grey wash was eliminated and the colours were

mixed with Chinese white powder before being applied to a pencil or ink sketch, giving them an opacity approximating that of oil paints. In the aquatint process, used when time was not a factor, an etching was printed in brown ink sepia — and the watercolours were then applied to the print. For the most part, the military topographers used muted colours — India ink, sepia, Prussian blue, gamboge and lake — for landscapes and stronger colours — cobalt, chrome yellow, carmine and various combinations of them — for man-made objects.

171

View of Kingston, looking over the Dock Yard from Fort Henry; 1833

Lt. E. C. Frome, R.E.; pen and ink drawing
The Agnes Etherington Art Centre, Queen's University at Kingston

At Kingston, four and a half miles below Kingston Mills, the Cataraqui waters flowed into Lake Ontario, 123 miles from the Bytown entrance to the canal. Military strategists viewed Kingston as the key to the defence of Upper Canada. It sat at the head of the St. Lawrence transport system and was the terminus of the Rideau Canal, as well as the principal supply depot for naval and military stores in the upper province, and the site of the naval dockyard.

In 1783 a British military force had been sent to the site of an old abandoned French fort, Fort Frontenac, to prepare for the settlement of Loyalist refugees from the newly independent United States of America. The first Loyalists began to arrive at Kingston in June 1784 and within three decades the town had a population of 1000 and about 150 homes, several shops and taverns, and number of warehouses erected by merchants engaged in the St. Lawrence forwarding trade and supplying the inland British garrisons. There was also an army barracks and a Commissariat depot, and the Provincial Marine, which was responsible for maintaining military transport vessels and warships on the Great Lakes, had established an arsenal and dockyard on Point Frederick.

No buildings stood on Point Henry until the War of 1812 when the army erected two stone blockhouses, connected by earth and log breastworks, and stationed 4000 troops there for the defence of Kingston and the St. Lawrence. The Royal Navy took over the dockyard to prosecute the shipbuilding race with the Americans, and by the close of the war, Kingston was the principal military and naval centre in Upper Canada, a prosperous garrison

town, and a key transhipment point in the St. Lawrence transport system.

In this drawing, the artist is looking out from a high promontory of land, Point Henry, across Navy Bay to the Royal Dockyard on Point Frederick, a long narrow peninsula between Navy Bay and Kingston Harbour. A small, earth and log breastwork fort, Fort Frederick, stood on the tip of the peninsula (not shown) just above which are several vessels, the *Canada* and the *Wolfe,* which were still in frame at the close of the war.

The first building on the left is a storage building for spars, masts and sails, and the next is the "Stone Frigate" where rigging, stores and naval guns were kept. The remaining buildings consisted of storage sheds, a steam house for shaping ship ribs, a blacksmith's shop, joiner's shop, tar and oil storehouses, and several other storehouses.

On the Kingston Harbour side of the peninsula is a long series of rowhouses erected in 1822 for artificers, the naval hospital and, at the far right, the commissioner's house where the commander of the dockyard lived. The hulks on Navy Bay are the frigates that were built during the War of 1812. At the close of the war, they were dismasted and roofed with planks to protect them from the weather, but in 1831 the British Navy Board economized by eliminating all funds for preserving them and by 1833 they were suffering from neglect and rot. On the far side of Kingston Harbour is the town. By 1833 it had a population of just over 3000, a permanent garrison of over 1000 troops, and was the most populous town in Upper Canada. With the construction of the canal, Kingston

Mills of Kingston, looking over the dockyard from Fort Henry. 1833.

became even more strategically important as it commanded the southern end of the canal where military supplies, troops, and ordnance would have to be transhipped into lake vessels for forwarding to the frontiers of Upper Canada, but for several seasons transhipments of Rideau cargoes were made above Kingston. Once past Kingston Mills, the canal followed the Lake Ontario inlet through a marshland, where the river current kept a channel open, to Kingston harbour, but in dry seasons a rocky shoal about a mile below Kingston Mills lay under only three feet of water.

During the construction period, a coffer dam had been built so the shoal could be blasted, but it was not done owing to financial restraints at the end of the project. During low-water seasons steamboats plying the canal had to tranship their cargoes at Kingston Mills until a navigable channel around the shoal was discovered. In 1840 a straight channel was blasted through the shoal and the canal at last functioned as planned.

Fort Henry, Kingston; 1839

Captain H. F. Ainslie, 25th Regiment of Foot; watercolour, pen and ink
Public Archives of Canada, C-510

The recently constructed Fort Henry redoubt, on the heights of Point Henry, is viewed in this painting from Kingston looking across the harbour and the dockyard on Point Frederick. The steamboat, possibly the *Hunter,* is heading toward Lake Ontario, having passed through the Rideau Canal with several Durham boats in tow.

On the left waterfront can be seen the commissioner's house with the Union Jack and naval pennant flying on the dock in front of it, to the right behind a picket fence is the naval hospital, and farther right are the artificers' rowhouses. In the background is the Fort Henry redoubt with the west branch ditch extending down to Navy Bay. To the right of the redoubt are the Commissariat buildings erected at an earlier date, and an advanced sea battery, still under construction, overlooking Lake Ontario.

Although the Ordnance was anxious that work should proceed on fortifications at Kingston simultaneously with the construction of the Rideau Canal, this proved impossible. In September 1825 the Smyth Commission had proposed that Fort Henry be reconstructed in masonry, that existing sea batteries on either side of the harbour entrance be enclosed in the rear, and that three masonry towers be constructed on the perimeter of the dockyard to protect the harbour, dockyard and the terminus of the proposed canal.

Smyth estimated the project at £201,718, but in October 1827 Colonel Wright submitted plans for two additional towers to improve the security of the dockyard, bringing the total estimate to £219,649. Parliament approved a reduced Kingston estimate in 1828, but differences persisted at the Ordnance over the adequacy of the proposed defences and how their cost could best be reduced in keeping with the approved estimate.

In arguing for the construction of 50- by 150-foot locks on the Rideau, By had pointed out that the proposed Kingston defences would not protect the dockyard and the commissariat buildings on Point Henry from bombardment and proposed that they be removed to the security of the Ottawa River at Bytown. The decision to construct the Rideau Canal on a river steamboat scale eliminated any possibility of moving the dockyard, but did not decide the stores depot question.

The two Ordnance officers on the Kempt Committee examined the Kingston defences and concluded that the dockyard and Commissariat stores were indeed vulnerable to bombardment from the Kingston side of the harbour. They proposed that a ring of six casemated redoubts be built around the perimeter of the Kingston harbour-naval dockyard area at an estimated cost of £206,413.

In September 1829 a committee of Royal Engineers at the Ordnance reported in favour of constructing the ring of six redoubts, supported by six Martello towers, three new sea batteries, and a strengthened Point Frederick sea battery, all of which would have made Kingston the most strongly fortified position in North America. The 16 works would cost £273,000, exclusive of the land purchases.

The Treasury refused to accept any increase in the approved 1828 Kingston estimate, and a stalemate ensued until January 1832 when a compromise, involving the piecemeal construction of the works on separate estimates, enabled work to commence on the Fort Henry redoubt and an advanced sea battery on Point Henry. The redoubt was completed in 1836 and the sea battery in 1841, but the Treasury adamantly refused to approve any further expenditures for land purchases in Kingston.

Lieutenant Colonel Oldfield, then Commanding Royal Engineer for the Canadas, revived By's earlier proposal of moving the Commissariat depot to Bytown. However, in 1841 the Master General of the Ordnance, Sir George Murray, decided the stores depot should be an integral part of Fort Henry, and a casemated stores depot was constructed, on the site of the Commissariat buildings shown in this illustration, to connect the Fort Henry redoubt with the advanced sea battery.

No further defences were build at Kingston until 1846-48 when, at the height of the Oregon boundary crisis, the defences on the Lake Ontario approach to the Rideau Canal and the naval dockyard were strengthened by two Martello towers (the Murney Tower and the Shoal

Tower) and a sea battery (the Market Battery) on the Kingston side of the harbour, and two Martello towers (the Fort Frederick Tower and the Cedar Island Tower) on the Point Frederick side of the harbour.

Small towers were also built at the lower end of east and west branch ditches of the Fort Henry redoubt. These works were the last permanent fortifications constructed in the Canadian interior. Today a restored Fort Henry complex (Old Fort Henry) and the fortifications erected in 1846-48 remain, with the exception of the former Market Battery, as reminders of the strategic importance of Kingston and the Rideau Canal in a bygone era.

Epilogue

When the Rideau Canal opened in May 1832, Colonel By was confident that if tolls were kept low, the Ottawa-Rideau steamboat navigation would ultimately capture a large share of the trade of the continental interior. Initially, the Ordnance and several leading Upper Canada merchants shared By's view, but the Rideau Canal did not live up to such high expectations even during the golden years, 1835-47, when it was an integral component of the Canadian transport system.

By had argued that supplies which took 11 to 14 days to reach Kingston on the St. Lawrence bateaux navigation at a cost of £4. 10 per ton, could be forwarded on the Rideau steamboat system in 3¼ days at a cost of only £1.3 per ton. This rate was substantially lower than rates on the Erie Canal and, with low tolls, there was a distinct possibility that even the downtrade would resort to the Rideau system rather than risk shooting the rapids on the St. Lawrence. However, By's projection proved overly optimistic. Once the Ottawa-Rideau system was fully operational, steamboats were able to deliver freight from Montreal to Kingston in four to five days, but freight rates remained far higher than he had anticipated.

In its first two years of operation, the potential of the Rideau Canal was limited by the incomplete state of the canals on the Ottawa River. The Grenville, Chute à Blondeau and Carillon canals were not completed until 1834, and three of the Grenville locks were on the original gunboat scale which precluded the passage of steamboats. The state of the Grenville Canal did not affect the speed of transit as barges could be put through the narrower locks, but it necessitated stationing steamboats above and below the canal to tow the barges where otherwise a single steamboat would have sufficed, thus adding to transport costs. Far more costly was the Treasury's refusal to authorize any further sums for Canadian canal construc-tion, preventing the Ordnance from building the single lock required to pass the Ste. Anne's Rapids at the confluence of the Ottawa and St. Lawrence rivers. This resulted in a monopoly being established by the Ottawa Steamboat Company, which constructed a lock at Vaud-reuil to bypass the Ste. Anne's Rapids. The company maintained artificially high freight rates by its control over the Vaudreuil lock and, after the provincial government opened a lock at Ste. Anne's in 1843, by entering into price-fixing agreements with the St. Lawrence forwarders who switched to the Rideau route.

Consequently, it cost £3.3.6 to ship a ton of freight on the Ottawa-Rideau route as opposed to only £2.4.4 a ton on the Erie system. The higher rates as well as cost advantages reaped by shippers using the port of New York rather than Montreal, doomed any hope the Rideau Canal might have had of siphoning off traffic from the Erie Canal.

The Rideau Canal, as expected, did enjoy a decisive advantage over the unimproved St. Lawrence River naviga-tion. As soon as the Ottawa canals were opened, a large proportion of the import trade passed through the Rideau system and the St. Lawrence was gradually abandoned by upbound freight. The St. Lawrence forwarders sent their barges to Kingston via Bytown, but preferred to risk shooting the St. Lawrence rapids on the return voyage as it took only two to three days to reach Montreal and avoided the tolls and towing charges.

As a result, a triangular trade system developed. Durham boats and barges were loaded with merchandise, salt or immigrants at Montreal and towed by relays of steamboats up the Ottawa River and through the Rideau Canal to Kingston, where the cargo and passengers were transferred into lake vessels. The barges, laden with wheat, flour and potash, were then sent back to Montreal on the St. Lawrence River with the aid of steam tow boats on the long navigable stretches between the rapids. In effect, the Rideau Canal complemented rather than competed with the St. Lawrence: the Rideau dominated the uptrade and the St. Lawrence the downtrade.

As the Ordnance had anticipated, the settlement of the Rideau corridor was facilitated by the opening of the canal and settlement in turn fostered trade along the canal. By 1836 the population stood at just over 24,800 and continued to increase steadily until 1861 when it stablized at 61,900. The settlers produced potash and wheat for export, and shipped barrels of beer, cider, whiskey, pork, ham, dried peas, flour and cheese to the Ottawa Valley lumber camps.

Lumbermen began to work the hitherto inaccessible Rideau Lakes-Perth area, rafting squared timber, as well as oak staves for barrel making, down the canal to Bytown. A heavy demand also arose for sawn lumber for export to the United States where the eastern forests were being rapidly depleted. Sawn lumber and saw logs were initially floated, and later barged, down the Rideau Canal to Kingston and beyond to the New York market via the Erie Canal.

For a short period during the boom years of the early 1840s, the Rideau Canal paid its own way, realizing Ordnance hopes that it would someday be self-supporting. But the hope of capturing a greater volume of the import-export trade soon evaporated. In 1848 the government of the Canadas, in a further effort to wrest trade from the Erie Canal, opened a series of canals on the St. Lawrence. With the enlargement of the Lachine Canal and the completion of the Beauharnois, Cornwall and Williamsburg canals bypassing the upper St. Lawrence rapids, a nine-foot-deep steamboat navigation was in place from Montreal to Kingston. This was much more direct route than the Ottawa-Rideau system, and its 45-foot-by-200-foot locks accommodated the large lake steamboats. Forwarders immediately transferred their establishments to the St. Lawrence, and the Rideau Canal was relegated to being solely a regional system.

By was right in asserting the critical importance of constructing the Rideau Canal as a steamboat navigation. Schooners and sloops were rapidly giving way to steamboats as the major vessels of commerce, and the impracticability of constructing towpaths meant that sailing vessels would have encountered unacceptable delays in their passage through the Rideau system. But his argument that a navigation accommodating large steamboats would draw the export trade of the Great Lakes interior through the Rideau system and encourage the development of a large-scale import trade was totally unrealistic. Even if it had proved feasible, it would not have captured the trade of the continental interior as is evident from the fate of the St. Lawrence canals.

Although the St. Lawrence ship canals were greatly superior to the Erie barge canal system in carrying capacity, time of transit and transport costs, the Erie still dominated the trade of the interior owing to New York's predominance over Montreal. Ships departing from New York, on the open sea, reached Europe sooner than those sailing through the constricted waters of the lower St. Lawrence River and the gulf, and were not subject to the pilotage, steam towing and high insurance charges paid by vessels using the more dangerous northern route. The advantages of using New York were more than sufficient to offset the extra costs incurred on the Erie, and political developments of the mid-1840s, such as the ending of the British colonial preference system and the passing of the American Drawback Acts, reinforced the predominance of the Erie system.

By clearly had taken a much too narrow view. In effect, he had merely appropriated for the Rideau Canal the dream that dominated St. Lawrence merchants during the canal-building era and the railway boom that followed. Setting forth such grandiose hopes for the Rideau Canal was unfortunate as by mid-century it made the canal appear to be a failure, thereby obscuring its real commercial benefits.

There was never any doubt as to the canal's critical importance as a military transport system. Despite Parliament's refusal to approve the massive expenditures required to implement Wellington's defence strategy, the Ordnance continued to press for the construction of the fortifications and canals, and in the post-1832 period concentrated on strengthening the defences of the Rideau Canal. For almost two decades, the preservation of the Rideau communication remained the primary object of military planning as the military was confident of its ability to defend Upper Canada with the canal in operation. Hence, work was pushed forward on the Kingston fortifications and the Ordnance continued to seek authorization to complete the ring of redoubts and towers required to protect the dockyard and prevent enemy troops from cutting the Rideau communication by passing behind Fort Henry, beyond the range of its guns.

No action was taken on the interior defences of the canal until 1837-38 when, in the aftermath of the Upper and Lower Canadian rebellions, "Hunter's Lodges" began to organize irregular forces in the United States, raising the prospect of marauders destroying the canal works. Local militia units were called out to garrison the blockhouses By had erected, guardhouses were constructed at Jones Falls and the White Fish dam, and defensible lockmasters' houses were built at several isolated locksites. Further protection was afforded by the Fort Henry garrison, British regiments sent via the canal to strengthen the Upper Canadian defences, and a naval detachment rushed to Kingston to build up an establishment there. Although the Kingston dockyard had been closed in 1834 and the aging, War-of-1812 frigates and gunboats auctioned off, that had been only a temporary measure to save expenditures until proper defences could be constructed for the dockyard. Hence, in 1838, plans were made for the construction of up to 30 gunboats at Kingston, and several of the old gunboats were repurchased and placed in service until new ones could be launched.

Although Wellington's strategy was intended to eliminate any need to engage in a shipbuilding contest with the Americans for supremacy on the Great Lakes, the dockyard was still required to construct warships to protect the open-water approaches to Kingston, York (Toronto) and the Niagara peninsula, and the gunboats propelled by oar and sail that were counted on to protect convoys moving along the canal systems. However, as By had anticipated, armed commercial steamers proved far superior to the gunboats in the one major engagement — the Battle of the Windmill at Prescott in November 1838 — in which both moved troops and bombarded enemy forces. Their superiority was so pronounced that within two years the Admiralty scrapped its new gunboats in favour of constructing steam paddlesloops for naval patrols on the Great Lakes.

At this juncture, the wisdom of constructing the Rideau Canal sufficiently large to accommodate steamboats was also beyond dispute. Although the Duke of Wellington had initially opposed By's proposal, he became a strong advocate of the Rideau steamboat navigation, especially after the 1837-38 crisis. In re-assessing his 1819 defence plan in the post-1840 period, Wellington remarked that:

> However expensive the works upon the Rideau, nobody now doubts the wisdom of the plan, its efficacy, and above all, its economy.

Wellington recommended that the three small Grenville locks and the Lachine and Welland canals be enlarged to complete an uninterrupted steamboat navigation from Quebec to the upper Great Lakes. He was supported by the army and the Ordnance who shared his belief that the speed and facility of the water communications would be the critical element in the defence of Upper Canada should war break out.

Despite the revolutionary transformation in the speed and cost of transport, Wellington did not share By's belief that these advantages would enable the Royal Navy to attain control of Lake Ontario, and By's strategy of a mobile defence utilizing the speed of steamboats was ignored. Wellington continued to see the navy in a strictly subordinate role in support of army operations. He was particularly anxious that the Ordnance should undertake a canal from the Bay of Quinte to Lake Simcoe via the Trent River to provide a secure line of supply from Kingston to the rear of York independent of Lake Ontario.

For two decades after the opening of the Rideau Canal, Wellington's views dominated military thinking on the defence of Upper Canada. However, at the time of the Oregon crisis, 1845-46, when the United States threatened to go to war over the disputed territory, the Ordnance concluded that Kingston could not be successfully defended against a combined land and sea assault unless a large field army covered the land approaches and towers were erected to protect the dockyard from bombardment by steam warships. The refusal of successive British governments to authorize further expenditures for fortifications had left the land approaches open to attack, and the light harbour defences were inadequate against steam warships, which could venture closer to shore than sailing vessels without fear of being trapped by a lull in the wind or the strong prevailing wind blowing onshore.

To strengthen the water approaches to Kingston, the British government authorized the construction of four Martello towers and another sea battery, all of which could be erected relatively quickly and cheaply, but it dismissed out of hand any idea of constructing additional permanent fortifications at Kingston or elsewhere.

A recommendation that the Rideau Canal defences be strengthened by constructing a fortress at Bytown and Martello towers or blockhouses at the more vulnerable locksites was also ignored as the government undertook diplomatic initiatives to settle all outstanding differences with the United States. The military was left to evolve a viable defence strategy taking into account the impossibility of completing Wellington's fortifications programme.

A strictly land-oriented defence based on permanent fortifications, regardless of its cost, was now viewed as inadequate. When Wellington devised his strategy in 1819, Upper Canada and the American territories south of the Great Lakes were sparsely settled, heavily forested and penetrated by primitive roads or trails that were all but impassable for heavy ordnance and large armies. The routes by which an American army could effectively attack the Canadas were few and clearly defined, and the objectives of any such attack were equally few and obvious.

However, in subsequent years a tide of immigrants had swept into the American territories and Upper Canada, clearing the land and opening transportation systems. An American force could now bypass any fortifications that might be erected in Upper Canada. Any field position that a British army might take to protect the exposed frontier was vulnerable to being turned if the Americans were free to land anywhere along the shore and advance on existing roads to attack the British force from the rear. Hence, the Great Lakes could not be abandoned to the Americans.

The new plan worked out by Lord Cathcart, the Commander of the Forces in Canada, differed radically from Wellington's. Upper Canada was to be defended by a large field army and the Royal Navy, which was to secure supremacy on the Great Lakes. To offset potential American advantages in numbers and resources, British forces were to be fully prepared to take the offensive immediately. A rapid seizure of the lightly defended American forts and harbours on the lakes would deprive the Americans of their shipbuilding capabilities and delay American offensives until heavy reinforcements could be sent from England and rushed inland via the Ottawa-Rideau.

Steamboats were counted on to move the troops and supplies quickly inland from Quebec and Montreal, and to transport and protect the assault troops that were to descend on the American harbours. Steamboats would also transport the large field armies that had to be quickly switched from one threatened area to another to meet American attacks or to prevent American resources from being effectively marshalled to launch attacks. Cathcart recommended that the government arrange for the speedy arming of commercial steamers, or have steamboats constructed that could be readily converted into warships.

The mobile defence strategy adopted in 1845-46 was in all its ramifications basically the strategy that By had urged in 1826-27. Whatever the cost, By had been convinced that it was the most economical and effectual means of defending the Canadas. In making use of the Great Lakes, it negated the need for a costly network of interior canals west of Kingston, and by relying on mobile field armies to meet any attack, eliminated the cost of constructing the numerous permanent fortifications required to implement Wellington's plan. The key to By's strategy, and Lord Cathcart's two decades later, was that steamboat navigations provided the British forces with a speed of movement superior to that enjoyed by the Americans on their side of the lakes.

Where the defence of the Canadas was concerned, the decision to construct the Rideau Canal as a steamboat navigation was by far the most critical decision made by the British military in the post-War-of-1812 period, and that decision was made solely because of the foresight, perseverance and courage of Colonel By. He was a military strategist of uncommon vision who realized at a very early date that the introduction of steamboats would totally transform warfare.

In military strategy as in engineering practice, By was innovative, imaginative and, although strict in carrying out orders, nonetheless confident of his own judgment and abilities. Indeed, that the Rideau Canal was completed at all, let alone built as a steamboat canal, was due to his superior zeal, initiative and abilities.

Had the Rideau Canal not been completed, or had it been constructed as a small gunboat canal, the whole of the Ordnance's efforts at engineering the defence of the Canadas would have been for naught insofar as Upper Canada was concerned. Gunboats propelled by oar and sail were totally obsolete. Whatever the extra cost of the larger locks, they were of inestimable value to the military. It not only rendered Wellington's static strategy, insofar as it was implemented, far more viable, but it also enabled the military to adopt a more effective and far less costly plan: the long-forgotten mobile defence strategy that By had enunciated almost two decades earlier.

Despite the unquestioned military importance of the Rideau Canal, by mid-century the British government was anxious to turn the Ordnance canals on the Ottawa and Rideau over to the provincial government. With the opening of the St. Lawrence canals and the onset of an economic depression in the late 1840s, revenues declined to the point where deficits of from £8000 to £10,000 a year were being incurred, a burden that the British government was intent on shifting to the province as part of a general policy of reducing colonial military expenditures. In 1849, negotiations were undertaken to that end. The Ordnance insisted that any transfer agreement must bind the province to maintain the canals in an efficient state, grant free passage to troops and military stores, protect the positions of the canal workers, and preserve to the Ordnance the lands not required specifically for canal purposes. However, the Canadian government insisted on complete control over the canals and the inclusion of the Ordnance lands in any transfer. A stalemate ensued until February 1853 when Treasury ordered the Ordnance to give up the canals and lands, and on September 30, 1853, cut off all funds for operating the canals. The provincial government assumed the cost of operating the canals, and a provincial act ratified the transfer, which became effective on November 5, 1856.

In the spring of 1857, the Ordnance canals were taken over by the Board of Works for Upper and Lower Canada, and were operated thereafter by the federal Department of Public Works (1867-1879), the Department of Railways and Canals (1879-1936), and the Department of Transport (1936-1972). Commercial traffic on the Rideau declined rapidly after the First World War and by the 1930s pleasure boats accounted for most of its traffic.

An awakening interest in the canal as an historic entity culminated in a 1967 recommendation of the Historic Sites and Monuments Board of Canada that the Rideau Canal be declared of national historic significance and the existing structures and historical environment be preserved. In 1972 the Parks Branch of the Department of Indian Affairs and Northern Development assumed responsibility for operating the canal as a recreational waterway while preserving its historical integrity. Parks Canada, now a part of the Department of Environment, has become heavily engaged in preserving and restoring the canal and its military structures, as well as in developing a wide range of interpretative programmes. To date, interpretation centres have been established at Kingston Mills, Jones Falls, Merrickville and the Bytown Museum in Ottawa.

The Rideau Canal is the only North American canal dating from the canal-building era of the early 19th century that remains in operation with most of its original structures intact. It is fitting monument to Colonel John By who, in a tremendous feat of organizational and engineering skill, succeeded in constructing one of the major engineering works of the 19th century. His achievement ranks By deservedly among the leading engineers of the age, and reflects equally well on his engineering officers and overseers, contractors, sappers and miners, and labourers, who played no less critical roles in building the canal.

Bibliography

Allodi, Mary. *Canadian Watercolours and Drawings in the Royal Ontario Museum.* Royal Ontario Museum, Toronto, 1974. Vol. 1.

Barker, Edward John. *Observations on the Rideau Canal.* Office of the British Whig, Kingston, 1834.

Bush, Edward F. *The Builders of the Rideau Canal, 1826-32.* Manuscript Report Series No. 185. Parks Canada, Ottawa, 1976.
————— *Commercial Navigation on the Rideau Canal, 1832-1961.* Manuscript Report Series No. 247. Parks Canada, Ottawa, 1977. (Now available in History and Archaeology, No. 54 [1981], Ottawa.)

Canada. Department of Indian Affairs and Northern Development. Parks Canada. National Historic Parks and Sites Branch. *Historical Assets of the Rideau Waterway.* Ottawa, 1967.

Canada. Public Archives.
RG1, E12, Executive Council Records, Office Reports and Register
RG5, A1, Civil Secretary's Correspondence, Upper Canada Sundries
RG8, Series C, British Military and Naval Records
RG11, Department of Public Works, Vol. 183
MG13, WO44, Department of Ordnance, Canada
MG13, WO55, War Office, Ordnance Miscellanea, Engineer Papers
MG24, A12, Dalhousie Muniments

Connolly, T. W. J. *The History of the Corps of Royal Sappers and Miners.* Longman, Brown, Green and Longmans, London, 1855. 2 vols.

Dendy, John. "The Strategic Importance of Kingston: A Study of the Role played by the British Base at Kingston, Ontario, in the Defence of Canada, 1778-1854." M.A. thesis, Carleton University, Ottawa, May 1965.

Denison, William T. "A Detailed Description of Some of the Works on the Rideau Canal, and of the Alterations and Improvements made therein since the Opening of the Navigation." In Great Britain. Army. Corps of Royal Engineers, *Papers on Subjects Connected with the Duties of the Corps of Royal Engineers.* John Weale, London, 1839. Vol. 3.

————— "Rideau Dams." In Great Britain. Army. Corps of Royal Engineers, *Papers on Subjects Connected with the Duties of the Corps of Royal Engineers.* 2nd ed. John Weale, London, 1844. Vol. 2.

Frome, Edward. "Account of the Causes which led to the Construction of the Rideau Canal, connecting the Waters of Lake Ontario and the Ottawa; the Nature of the Communication prior to 1827; and a Description of the Works by means of which it is converted into a Steam-boat Navigation." In Great Britain. Army. Corps of Royal Engineers, *Papers on Subjects Connected with the Duties of the Corps of Royal Engineers.* 2nd ed. John Weale, London, 1844. Vol. 1.

George, V.A. "The Rideau Corridor: The Effect of a Canal System on a Frontier Region, 1832-1898." M.A. thesis, Queen's University, Kingston, 1972.

Hardie, Martin. *Water-colour Painting in Britain.* B. T. Batsford, London, 1967. Vol. 1: The Eighteenth Century.

Harper, J. Russell. *Paintings in Canada, A History.* University of Toronto Press, Toronto, 1966.

Hay Snyder, Marsha. *Nineteenth-Century Industrial Development in the Rideau Corridor: A Preliminary Report.* Manuscript Report Series No. 215. Parks Canada, Ottawa, 1977.

Heisler, John P. "The Canals of Canada." Canadian Historic Sites: Occasional Papers in Archaeology and History, No. 8 (1973). Ottawa.

Hill, Hamnet P. "The Construction of the Rideau Canal." *Ontario Historical Society: Papers and Records,* Vol. 22 (1925), pp. 117-24. Toronto.

Hitsman, J. Mackay. *Safeguarding Canada, 1763-1871.* University of Toronto Press, Toronto, 1968.

Hunter, Louis C. *Steamboats on the Western Rivers: An Economic and Technological History.* Octagon Books, New York, 1969.

Lavell, W. S. "The History of the Present Fortifications at Kingston." *Ontario Historical Society, Papers and Records,* Vol. 31 (1936), pp. 155-77. Toronto.

Legget, Robert F. *Canals of Canada.* Douglas, David and Charles, Vancouver, 1976.

————— "The Jones Falls Dam on the Rideau Canal, Ontario, Canada." *Transactions of the Newcomen Society,* Vol. 31 (1958), pp. 205-18. London.

————— *Ottawa Waterway: Gateway to a Continent.* University of Toronto Press, Toronto, 1975.

————— *Rideau Waterway.* University of Toronto Press, Toronto, 1967.

Mactaggart, John. *Three Years in Canada: An Account of the Actual State of the Country in 1826-7-8. Comprehending its Resources, Productions, Improvements, and Capabilities; and including Sketches of the State of Society, Advice to Emigrants, &c.* Henry Colburn, London, 1829. 2 vols.

Morgan, H. R. "The First Tay Canal: An Abortive Upper Canadian Transportation Enterprise of A Century Ago." *Ontario Historical Society, Papers and Records,* Vol. 29 (1933), pp. 103-6. Toronto.

————— "Steam Navigation on the Ottawa River." *Ontario Historical Society: Papers and Records,* Vol. 23 (1926), pp. 370-83. Toronto.

Parent, Jean-Claude. *Profil de certains édifices le long du canal Rideau.* Travail inédit No. 225. Parks Canada, Ottawa, 1977.

Passfield, Robert W. *Engineering the Defence of the Canadas: Lt. Col. John By and the Rideau Canal.* Manuscript Report Series No. 425. Parks Canada, Ottawa, 1980.

————— *Historic Bridges on the Rideau Waterways System: A Preliminary Report.* Manuscript Report Series No. 212. Parks Canada, Ottawa, 1976.

————— "Ordnance Supply Problems in the Canadas: The Quest for an Improved Military Transport System, 1814-1828." *HSTC Bulletin, Journal of the History of Canadian Science, Technology and Medicine,* Vol. 5, No. 3 (Nov. 1981). Toronto.

Price, Karen. *Construction History of the Rideau Canal.* Manuscript Report Series No. 193. Parks Canada, Ottawa, 1976.

Raudzen, George K. *The British Ordnance Department and Canada's Canals.* Wilfred Laurier University Press, Waterloo, 1979.

———— "The British Ordnance Department in Canada, 1815-55." Ph.D. dissertation, Yale University, New Haven, Conn., 1970.

Reid, Dennis. *A Concise History of Canadian Painting*. Oxford University Press, Toronto, 1973.

Ross, A. D. H. *Ottawa: Past and Present*. Musson Book Company, Toronto, 1927.

Saunders, Ivan J. "A History of Martello Towers in the Defence of British North America, 1796-1871." Canadian Historic Sites: Occasional Papers in Archaeology and History, No. 15 (1976), pp. 5-169. Ottawa.

Sneyd, Robert B. "The Role of the Rideau Waterway, 1826-56." M.A. thesis, University of Toronto, Toronto, 1965.

Stanley, G. F. G. "Historic Kingston and Its Defences." Ontario History, Vol. 46, No. 1 (Winter 1953), pp. 21-35. Toronto.

Steppler, Glenn A. "A Duty Troublesome Beyond Measure: Logistical Considerations in the Canadian War of 1812." M.A. thesis, McGill University, Montreal, 1974.

Stevenson, David. *Sketch of the Civil Engineering of North America, Comprising Remarks on the Harbours, Rivers and Lake Navigation, Lighthouse, Steam Navigation, Water-Works, Canals, Roads, Railways, Bridges, and Other Works in the Country*. John Weale, London, 1838.

Strickland, William. *Report on Canals, Railways, Roads and other Subjects made to "The Pennsylvania Society for the Promotion of Internal Improvements."* H.C. Carey and I. Lea, Philadelphia, 1826.

Tulloch, Judith. *The Rideau Canal, 1832-1914*. Manuscript Report Series No. 177. Parks Canada, Ottawa, 1975. (Now available, as "The Rideau Canal: Defence, Transport and Recreation," in History and Archaeology, No. 50 [1981], Ottawa.)

Wilson, Arnold. *A Dictionary of British Military Painters*. F. Lewis, Leigh-on-Sea, England, 1972.

Wylie, William N.T. *Elements of a Military Heritage: A Structural History of the Merrickville and Newboro Blockhouses, the Jones Falls and Whitefish Guardhouses, and the Jones Falls Defensible Lockmaster's House*. Manuscript Report Series No. 372. Parks Canada, 1980.
———— "Transience and Poverty: A Study of the Rideau Canal Construction Workers, 1826-32." Manuscript on file, Ontario Region, Parks Canada, Cornwall, 1981.